Welcome Into My Mind

Based on a true story of a little girl who lost her ability to relate
to the real world around her due to a devastating tragedy
and how she overcame every mental struggle to succeed in life.

MARY HANNAH BILGER

*Dedicated to the loving memory of
my Uncle Harry and Aunt Lina Watson.
Knowing you are loved by someone makes all the difference.*

Table of Contents

Chapter 1

"It can't be real."

I stared into my mother's terrified face and heard my Aunt Theresa's hysterical moaning. "Oh my God, oh my God."

They both ran for the front door, and I was left looking at my blue Huffy bicycle. Just the day before I carried it up the two flights of stairs and managed to carefully wedge it into the closet. The closet door was now open. With my aunt out of the way, I could see the lump. Only the night before that form had been my father.

I couldn't turn away fast enough. As I did a sharp one-eighty, my eyes connected with our big mirror hanging on the wall. I couldn't turn away. My feet were anchored to the floor. I saw my face, but somehow it wasn't me. The Mary in the mirror calmly told me to scream. I just kept staring at her. She said again, "Mary, SCREAM!"

Yes, I had to agree with the ten-year-old, brown-eyed girl looking back at me from the mirror. A scream was necessary. I calmly walked out the front door of our apartment and let out a blood-curdling scream that could be heard in heaven or hell. I had no idea at that moment, that I would never be that little girl again. I was no longer in the here and now. I was an observer looking in, numb and cold. I moved on autopilot.

"It was real."

I just couldn't believe it. A startled Mrs. Cyr finally answered the door to my mother's pounding and Aunt Theresa's crying. As we all burst into her apartment, my sobbing mother said to the little woman, "He's dead, call the police!"

"What if the police think I did it," my shaking and hysterical aunt kept saying.

There was chaos all around us now.

"Get them some blankets before they go into shock."

"I hear the sirens now," someone else said.

I just stood there. I wasn't crying like my mom. I wasn't shaking like my aunt. I was numb. I was watching all of this happen. It was like it was happening to someone else. If only this was a movie where the director would say, "Cut," or if I didn't want to see any more, I could just turn off the TV.

They had me wait in my bedroom, not at Mrs. Cyr's place. I sat on my full-sized bed with the blue headboard. My pajamas were still on my bed from getting dressed so fast. I looked across the room at my little table and chairs, with my dolls waiting for me to pour tea. I was ten, but I still loved my dolls.

Quite a bit of time had passed before a tall man dressed in regular clothes came into my room. His voice was very soft when he asked me my name. I answered, "Mary Falkenburg." I didn't say my middle name Hannah, because I thought it was an ugly name.

"Were your mom and dad fighting last night?" the nice man wanted to know.

"No. We watched television and I went to bed at eight o'clock."

"Did you hear anything last night after you went to bed?"

"Yes. A loud noise woke me up," I calmly explained to him.

"What did you think it was Mary?"

"I thought it was the silver coffee set that had fallen off the counter in the kitchen."

He then told me to tell him everything I could remember since I woke up that morning. That morning was Dec 14, 1959.

"Well, my mom woke me up earlier than usual for school. She told me that she couldn't find my dad, which sounded crazy to me. She told me to get dressed and run to Aunt Theresa and Uncle John's and see if Daddy was there," I explained.

This new "poor living," as my mother called it, did not allow us to have a telephone. But it was just a five-minute walk to my aunt and uncle's place. Mom had to stay at our place because of my two little brothers, Ed and Dave.

"She told me, 'If your dad isn't there ask her to come back here with you. Tell her there was no note saying he was going any place and the car is still parked out front.'"

I had put my coat on in my bedroom so Mom couldn't see that I had on the new pink dress she had bought me. I walked fast through the complex of apartment buildings. The new pink dress was pretty but it sure wasn't warm. Each building looked exactly like the one in front of it. I wasn't worried about my father. We were pals and I loved him with my whole heart. I knew he would be back soon, from wherever he had gone.

I told the officer he wasn't at my aunt's. "I waited while she put her coat on and we came right back."

Mom was still pacing the floor, as she had been when I left. Mom and Aunt Theresa sat on our bizarrely colored green and yellow couch made of messy threads. They were trying to make sense of what was going on.

"Christine," my aunt said, "you know Ed is always playing tricks with the kids and doing magic tricks for them. Maybe he is just hiding and waiting to pop out at them when they get up."

"Aunt Teresa got up from the couch, walked over to the closet, and turned the handle," I finished.

The nice officer wanted to know what I saw when I looked in the closet, but the funny thing was, I didn't feel like I was talking about my father. How could I casually say, "My daddy was slumped over my bicycle, dead"? The police officer left a few moments later.

A woman came into my room. I don't remember who, but they led me out the front door and across the hall to Mrs. Cyr's apartment.

3

Although the door was unlocked, Mrs. Cyr must have gone to work because her apartment was empty.

I think it was the pretty lady who lived upstairs. She thought I should be out of our apartment while the police did their job. She was new to "poor living" also. The pretty lady had blonde hair and always looked nice.

She left me at the Cyr's apartment and said she would be back later to check on me. But she didn't come back to check on me. No one came to check on me. Hour after hour I lay on that couch and watched the clock tick. I wasn't hungry. I wasn't thirsty. I wasn't tired, nor did I want to walk back across the hall to our place. I just waited. I was satisfied to lay there and do nothing.

"Nothing."

"Nothing," was the word that was making its way into my little heart. I didn't think about anything. I didn't replay what I saw over and over. I laid there and thought of nothing. I had no way of knowing that one little word would someday help save my life. For now, it summed up how I was dealing with things. Feelings were beyond me at that time, thank goodness. I don't think I would have been able to process that I had just looked at my dead father's body, been questioned about his death, then taken to a place I had never been in before and left there, the entire day, by myself. By myself! All day, all alone, at a neighbor's apartment.

Late that afternoon my Aunt Nell came storming in to get me. She was still in her white uniform from work as a nurse. Aunt Nell was affectionally known for hugging and kissing us kids until we would fall in a heap. Today I could see something different in her big, caring eyes. She was really mad.

"Come on honey, let's get you home," she said, as she put her big arms around me and walked me back across the hall. The place was full of people.

I have very little memory of the days that followed. But some decisions needed to be made immediately on whether to tell my grandmom and grandpop, who lived in Tuckerton, New Jersey, about how their only child died.

Mom decided to call their doctor for advice. He said, "Christine, I don't think their hearts could handle knowing that Ed took his own life. Why don't we tell them he died in a car accident?"

I guess it was easy to get away with a lie like that back in 1959, because that was exactly what the doctor told them.

"Mary, it's important that your grandparents don't learn how daddy died," my mother said. I knew I would have no trouble keeping that secret because I had one of my own. I believed that my dad's death was my fault. I finally ran the scene over and over in my mind until I thought I would throw up. There was no other explanation that I could come up with.

Dad had started taking turns with me doing the evening dishes. "Daddy, take my turn for me tonight, please, please, please," I begged.

There seemed like a mountain of pots. I would have been in that kitchen forever. He finally said, "Sure, you go play" with a small smile on his face.

Why had I been so selfish that night? I hadn't thought of him at all, only my selfish, little self. I probably made him mad. He would be with me now if I had thought of him, instead of me. I went to Sunday school every week. I knew the rules. I had disappointed him. I was selfish and he didn't love me anymore. That's why he was dead.

"Daddy died because of me," I whispered.

Mom wrapped me in her arms. "Oh honey," my mom cried. "You're daddy's little girl and there is nothing he wouldn't do for you. Remember how he always told you the moon was yours, but you had to share it with everyone? He always made a point of telling you how he was going to go up there and polish it when the moon was small. Then when the moon was full again, he would take you outside to show you what he had done, for you."

I stayed quiet. Mom looked me in the eyes. "Mary, your daddy is dead because he lost his job and he couldn't take care of us. He couldn't live with that."

I wanted to know why he thought I could live without him.

Chapter 2

I tried to hold onto the good memories. My childhood had been nothing but good. We lived on Spiegel Avenue in Verga, New Jersey. It was a cute-looking house that went straight back. No curves of any kind. One room right after the other.

The driveway was on the left of the house and went straight back to the fence. I had my wonderful backyard that kept my dog Poochie from roaming the streets, looking for treats. The Jungle Gym had an acrobat bar that my friends and I could swing upside down on. But my most prized possession, the one that I received from one of my big birthday parties, was my very own pool.

I think I gave them a hint that I wanted one the day I rounded up the kids in the neighborhood. We all got shovels and started digging up my backyard. We were sure we could have a pool by the end of the day. That was not one of my better ideas. My parents yelled a little and shook their heads saying, "Where does she get these ideas?"

Our house had an enclosed sunporch with windows all around. Big, burgundy furniture filled the room. I would curl up in those chairs with the warm sun on me and read my books. In the afternoons I would kneel on the chair to look over the back. I'd wait for daddy to come home. Often, he would have something for me.

"Ed, you're spoiling her," was the comment that usually followed from Mom. He would agree with her and wink at me.

Mom walked me to the corner to catch the bus for school every morning. She was involved with my school life. Mom belonged to the PTA and kept in contact with my teacher. My cousin Diane, my very best friend in the whole world at the time, was in my class. I was so excited. I could see her every day. I loved school. I always had pretty clothes to wear, and Mom worked hard to beat my curls into submission every morning. She always won, no matter how much I complained that it hurt.

When school was finished for the day, Mom could be counted on to be waiting at the corner to walk me back home. She didn't like me to walk with the little girl that lived two houses away from us. She never told me why, but she made sure I stayed away from her. She was like a hawk, always looking, always protecting. I knew I was loved, but where I could win dad over with my toothless smile, Mom was very different.

"No missy, those big brown eyes are not going to work on me. I said no and that is the end of it." And I knew it was.

My mom's side of the family made up for my dad not having any siblings, just his mom and dad. My mom was the baby of the Foster family. She had two older brothers and three older sisters. My mom's sister, Aunt Lina and her husband Uncle Harry, were my very favorites. We saw each other almost every day. They were always taking me home with them. One day they got in trouble for that.

I was playing in the yard one summer day. Uncle Harry thought it would be funny if they put me in their car to sneak me away. They only did that once. I got a loud introduction to, "Don't go anywhere without telling Mom!"

Aunt Nell looked exactly like my mom in her face. She was just bigger in size. She wasn't around us as much as the other aunts. She worked a lot. I think Aunt Nell was married before and divorced that husband. Uncle Lou, her current husband, was a widower. His wife left him with three girls and one boy to raise. I found out that I could learn a lot by sitting in a corner and being really quiet. I learned that one of Uncle Lou's girls was named Theresa. My mother's brother, John, eventually married Theresa. So that made his sister, his mother-in-law. It was the funniest thing I ever heard.

But the best part of the family was the cousins. We couldn't wait for a party or a visit so we could all be together. Life was full of fun, and we had a feeling of belonging to each other.

My younger brother Ed was born when I was four. I was so glad to see him come along. Up until then, I was sleeping in the crib. I was very small for four but big enough to know I wanted a big girl bed. Boy, did I get one. The size of it was huge. The beautiful blue headboard, oh my, it dazzled. And the official name for the bed, "The Hollywood Bed," made me think that God must really love me.

Now, instead of being in the crib myself, I could go in and watch Ed sleep. My new baby brother was so beautiful. All I wanted to do was hold him. But Ed didn't get to be the baby for long. Dave was born when Ed was two. But he didn't come home from the hospital for a long time. Mom said he was very sick. I didn't understand the problems but when Mom asked me to bow my head and pray hard for my baby brother, I instinctively knew he must be very sick. His kidneys were not functioning correctly. It took a long time for the doctors to make him better. But our prayers worked. Now we were a happy family of five. My life was happy. Then Dad lost his job as a boat engineer. Everything changed.

Things went from good, to bad, to hurtful. We were finally forced to live with my mother's parents, grandma and grandpa Foster. They were old and obviously could not tolerate kids. We lived with them for a year after Dad lost his job. Grandfather Foster was an alcoholic. He was a very mean alcoholic, so going into public assisted living felt like a step up from where we were.

We moved to Westfield Acres in Camden, New Jersey. It was twenty-five acres of red brick apartment buildings that were three stories high. There were over five hundred families that lived there. For a kid that meant wherever you went, there was someone to play with. It was hilly, so that was perfect for bike riding. It was laid out where vehicles could not drive through. You had to park on the outside roads and walk in. We lived way in the back on the second floor.

It was July when we moved in. My brother Ed's birthday was July 21st. Two days later would be my birthday. The first day that we moved in, Mom sat on the old, dark brown tiled floor. Ed and I sat on the floor across from her. She had a suitcase laying on the floor between us, where she put two chocolate Tasty Cakes, each with a candle in it.

"Mom wants you kids to know I can't give you a birthday party this year. Dad isn't working, and we can't afford it. Mom will make it up to you next year."

She was always so funny when she would talk to us. She never said "I". It was always "Mom". When talking to others she would always refer to me as "my Mary," as if everyone had one of their own. Hearing that always warmed my heart. Dad did get a few jobs, but they took him out of town, and they didn't last very long.

One time, things got so bad my mom had to call her brother Bud to bring us groceries. Uncle Bud and Aunt Alice lived right across the street from us for a short time when we lived on Spiegel Avenue. After Mom called Uncle Bud, he started stopping by regularly to make sure we had groceries. Other members of the family did the same thing. Whenever my Uncle Harry made tapioca pudding, he always brought us a big bowl of it. They did as much as they could for us.

My parents were in public assisted housing, but they would not, under any circumstances, go on welfare. My mom knew everything about financial assistance, but my dad just couldn't tolerate the idea of welfare. They treated welfare like a cuss word.

But we managed. And it wasn't all bad. For one thing, I had an aunt and uncle and eight cousins that lived in the front of Westfield Acres. My Aunt Theresa was also my godmother. She was short and stocky with bright, natural, red hair and a face full of freckles. I loved going to her house.

My cousin Betty Ann was so lucky because she lived in a building that had an arch. That was a building where the apartments were on the left and right, and it arched in the middle. It didn't have first-floor apartments in the center like most of the buildings. On rainy days I would go up to play with Betty, Bob, and Jack. We would play "Red

Rover". Or maybe a game of "Kick the Can". Mr. Sample's store was also under the first arch. He sold newspapers, candy, and lots of cigarettes. He was always busy. I don't know how he did it, but he worked by himself, and he was blind. I didn't try it, but they said if you gave him a five and told him it was a ten, he would know the difference.

All the buildings were the same except for the number of bedrooms. They did have one redeeming quality. They had big windows in every room that let in a lot of sunshine. Mom painted our apartment light green, better to show off her messy, lime green and yellow couch. Mom also wore orange shoes. None of my friends' moms wore orange shoes. Mom was very different that way too.

She was pretty but she wasn't small. She was 5'7" and probably weighed one hundred and sixty pounds. Mom had the most beautiful complexion. Unfortunately, she had some moles on her face that she would eventually have removed. My father, on the other hand, was much shorter than my mother. He had curly dark hair and deep blue eyes.

My grandmother and grandfather Falkenburg, on my dad's side, were very small. Grandmom was five feet even. A little wind would have blown her away. She had pure white, curly hair. Her pearls were always around her neck. Not one time did she ever yell at me. She would talk to me in a way that made me feel sorry for whatever I'd done wrong, but never did she raise her voice at me.

The same thing held true for my grandfather. He was great. He had this old car that all the guys wanted to buy. Daddy said, "Thank goodness everyone recognizes that car and gives him a wide berth. I wish he would sell it."

No chance, Grandpop loved that car. "Old as dirt," was how my father described it.

They lived one block from what they referred to as "my lake." It had a beautiful sandy beach, with lots of trees for shade. The sand was the color of gold. Not white, but gold. It made the water shimmer yellow.

Of course, I wanted to go swimming all the time. Sometimes, when I was out driving with Grandpop, he would take me for a quick swim with no bathing suit and no towel. He just let me drip-dry in my shorts.

I was told that the Falkenburg family, several generations past, were the founding fathers of Tuckerton. Someone showed it to me in a book once. I know they were treated with a great deal of respect.

My father was thirty-five when he married my mother, who was twenty-five at the time. I looked at their wedding pictures whenever I had a chance. The pictures showed Mom wearing a long white gown. Her veil looked as if it was flowing from a crown. They looked so beautiful and happy.

Chapter 3

When dad died on December 14, we didn't have a Christmas tree. I knew no presents were bought. Being ten years old, I didn't believe in Santa Claus, but I loved everything about Christmas. The TV specials and the holiday decorations. The excitement of Christmas Eve. I loved singing Christmas carols to the boys with the lights out, except for a little Santa that lit up red. They were all happy smiles and that made me happy too. We didn't have too many traditions.

Mom would make the eggnog that everyone hated except her. The nuts and fruits had to be out on the coffee table the whole week of Christmas. Our past Christmases were always a very special time. But that Christmas of 1959 left me with only one memory. No parents. We wouldn't dare to go into the living room to open gifts without Mom and Dad. But my oh-so-loving Aunt Lina and Uncle Harry took us all to their house on Christmas Eve. Our cousins Skip and Eddie woke us up early. Into the living room we all ran on Christmas morning.

Ed, Dave, and I watched as they opened their gifts. I noticed there was one gift for Ed, and one for Dave and me. But what I remembered so well was the smile and happiness I saw on my brothers' faces. I was so glad they could experience happiness instead of the emptiness I was living inside. I have no memory of seeing my mother that day. But I'm sure she was there, her hands wrapped around a hot cup of coffee.

We rang in the new year of 1960 with me, Dave, and Ed huddled in Mom's bed with her. We listened to fireworks. I felt Mom's nervousness and sorrow as she talked to me that night. I thought she looked beautiful with her dark hair against the white pillowcase, which was so easy to see with the moon as bright as it was through the window. She was on one side of the bed and the boys were between us.

"Mary, we're going to be ok. I know I haven't been myself lately, and I'm sorry."

I knew she had been to the doctor several times for her nerves, as she put it. We drifted off to sleep when someone decided to ring in the new year by firing a gun. My heart pounded. We finally went back to sleep, shaking.

When I returned to school, I felt awkward and kind of ashamed. If anyone started talking about my father's death, I would change the subject as soon as I could. I never heard of a father killing himself. I thought everyone looked at me differently. I knew I felt different. I felt scared and vulnerable.

Dad's social security check started coming in for us kids. Mom got a separate one for herself. That helped a lot. At least Mom could stay home and take care of us. But everything was so different now. I was stranded in a different life. The change happened so fast. One day I was a ten-year-old girl, then the next day, it felt like I was an adult, responsible for almost everything. Instead of going out to play with my friends, I had to take the boys out to play. Not play with them but be responsible for them.

"Mary, take your brothers outside for a while and don't you dare let anything happen to them. You are responsible," Mom said in a very harsh voice.

I had come to dread hearing her voice.

"Mommy, why are you so mean?" I finally got up enough nerve to ask.

"If I didn't love you, I wouldn't care what you do."

Her answer didn't make any sense to me. It wasn't worth two cents.

I was taught how to iron and how to scrub the bathroom, which were now my new jobs. And of course, I was responsible for the dishes. I had been doing those for a long time. But now it was without the help of dad. Even my loving aunts said I should be helping more. But it wasn't an issue of helping out. If one of the boys fell and hurt himself, it was my fault. If someone came over to the house and the house was messy, it was my fault. I couldn't do anything right. I just wanted to yell, "I'm only ten years old!"

When I was eleven years old, Ed was seven and Dave was five. Mom decided, probably because Dad died in the place, to move us to the front of the Westfield Acres. She moved us into a two-bedroom apartment, and it was on the third floor. Even I knew that didn't make any sense, but Aunt Theresa lived in that building and I guess she just wanted to be closer to her.

The move was horrific. I carried box after box up to the new place on the third floor, along with all the other helpers Mom had put together. But when it came time to empty the five-gallon fish tank by myself, because it was mine and therefore my responsibility, I did the best I could. On the walk up the stairs, I stumbled, and the fish that I had very carefully put in the bucket were now all up and down the stairs, flopping all over. I tried to save them, but I was stepping on some while trying to save the others. I just couldn't do it.

I cleaned the mess up and flushed the fish down the toilet. It was something else that I loved and lost. The fish were one of the last things my dad had given me. It brought tears to my eyes, but I was able to push the hurt away. I was getting pretty good at doing that lately.

That year I was invited to attend a summer camp sponsored by our church at Wildwood, New Jersey. I was so excited. I hadn't been down to the shore since dad had taken us a long time ago. A whole week of sun and fun, I couldn't wait. My Aunt Lina had taken me shopping and I had a suitcase full of new clothes. Mom always kept us well dressed and I loved, loved, loved pretty clothes. Those last few weeks before I left went by so slowly.

It turned out that "summer camp" was a big, beautiful house close to the ocean. Upon arriving, I overheard the woman in charge ask one of the counselors to sit me and another little girl at her table for meals. For some reason, that just warmed my heart hearing that. I slept well that night, but the next morning I felt strange. I wasn't enjoying listening to the girls giggling or joining the games. The games seemed so silly to me. I felt like I didn't belong. I was much more comfortable being with the counselors in the house. I would help with the chores until they took me by my hand and made me go out to play. They told me, "Go have some fun, Mary."

It was a grand place, and everyone was always in a good mood. The last night at camp there was a big party that everyone attended. Mrs. Green, the woman in charge, gave a speech and told us how much she enjoyed having us there. Each counselor said a little something about how happy they were to be there. The last person to speak was Mrs. Green again.

"Each year we give an award called, 'The best girl at camp award'. Every councilor cast a vote for their choice. I am happy to announce this year's winner is Mary!"

Everyone clapped and smiled at me. My heart swelled. What an exciting feeling. I didn't even know there was a contest, but I won! I was smiling from ear to ear as I walked to the front in my pretty yellow dress with little dogs on it, to collect my award. I thanked them from the outside and I thanked Jesus from the inside.

I couldn't wait to get home and show Mom. I went into the house. With great care, I took the bubble wrap off the little ceramic angel that I had won. I walked into the living room with such pride and showed her.

"Mom, look! I won 'the best girl at camp award' for being a good helper and good girl at camp," I beamed at her.

She looked straight into my face and said, "They don't know you very well, do they?"

My throat dried up. Why was she being like this? I hadn't been home in a week. I knew I couldn't have done anything to make her angry at me. I staggered backward as if she had landed a punch straight to my face. The blow didn't land in my heart. It landed smack in my brain. I tightened my lips. This was where I drew the line.

I was done being her good girl. Childhood had come to an official close for me that day. Nothing was ever going to be the same. I would take care of myself. The only time I could remember being this upset, was when I was watching Danny Thomas on television a few months back. He was singing a song about "Daddy's little girl". I broke down and cried my heart out. I sobbed and sobbed until I had cried out every single ounce of love and feeling that I had for my father. Because he had done this to me. His choice. He was the selfish one.

My tears were cathartic. I rarely spoke or thought of him after that day. And now my mother was gone as far as I was concerned. Nothing would hurt my heart again. I wouldn't let it. I dealt with everything out there on the surface. I could face the world out there with my guard up. Nothing mattered out there. I could be, do, say, and act in any way that was necessary. But nothing, nothing, would ever hurt me again.

A few months later grandpop Falkenburg died in his sleep. A couple of months after that my precious grandmother followed him to the grave. Within six months my dad and his parents were all gone. But I was safe. I could handle it. And I did.

No one knew I was operating from my surface. My heart was locked away in a private closet. There were layers and layers of protection and the tiniest key, for the lock. I flung the key to my heart away into the deepest depths of the big, blue ocean. But I still possessed a vulnerability that only fear could cause.

Chapter 4

I believe my oldest memory is TI58358. I knew that telephone number before I could count to twenty. With that number came instant help, unconditional love, and always a feeling of happiness. That number belonged to the Watson family, to Aunt Lina and Uncle Harry. I had to recite that number for my parents on a regular basis for fear that I would forget it. I never did.

My Aunt Lina and Uncle Harry were the prominent two people in my life after my parents. I loved them as much as I loved my mom and dad. I wanted to be around them all the time. They were fun and they always made me feel special. I knew they loved me too. Everybody liked to be around them.

Anytime they came over, I was ready to go. There was always room for one more at their house. They had a son and daughter, Little Harry and Barbara Ann, both older than me. Then came Skip. Their youngest was named Eddie, and he was born the same year as my brother Ed. Pure joy is what I felt whenever I would see them, which was often, thank goodness.

Skip and I were the closest in age. We loved playing and we never got tired of being outside. Our imaginations were our toys. We could round up the bad guys and have them in jail before lunch. As we got older, the games progressed to baseball and badminton. But we never stopped climbing that big, old apple tree in Aunt Lina and Uncle Harry's yard.

"Mary, let me put your hair in a French twist," Barbara Ann asked one day. "You would look so pretty with your hair up and makeup on."

Barbara Ann was sixteen. I was torn between wanting to go swimming with Skip or having Barbara Ann help me look better. Barbara was starting to win that debate. This teenager was willing to spend time with a twelve-year-old. And oh my, I loved it.

She would practice the latest hairstyles and the newest makeup colors on me. It was so transforming. I would walk in as a plain twelve-year-old going on thirteen. When she was done with me, I couldn't stop staring in the mirror. I looked so different.

"Could that girl really be me?"

I could easily pass for sixteen, if not older. Which I proved to myself when I got home. One of the older girls in the neighborhood didn't recognize me. "Wow, Mary you look great!" She had a stunned look on her face. I could tell right then that I definitely looked older than 12.

Another time, I was on my way to the Hoagie Shop. I had been in that place or passed by it almost daily. It was an exciting day at our house, which was usually the first of the month when Mom got our checks. She would send me over to buy hoagies for dinner. But this time when I walked in, the guys noticed. And I mean all of them. The attention was heady stuff to experience. Unfortunately, Mom noticed too. But I was hooked. I wanted more.

"Mary, you're too young to wear makeup and do your hair up like that. Go wash your face. And don't ever let me catch it on you again," Mom ordered.

In the past, I would've never thought to disobey her. Now I didn't care. I just had to figure out a way to make it happen without getting caught. When I went to Aunt Lina's house for a weekend, I would always ask Barbara Ann if she had any old makeup she didn't want. She had everything you could imagine. I thought she was wonderful.

Barbara Ann was a good teacher. She taught me the right colors for my complexion. She taught me how to apply just enough eye makeup to look good but not too much. I had inherited my mother's complexion and the Falkenburg's slight build from my father's side. But with a slight build came no boobs. I think every girl I knew had boobs except me. I was twelve and I wanted boobs. Heck, I was still wearing undershirts. I wish I had known about putting a sock in a bra back then, but I didn't. Oh, well. I would make myself into a flat-chested beauty. The only bad part was having to sneak around Mom to put the make-up on.

But it wasn't too hard to get out of the house with the stuff I needed because I carried an old fashion briefcase which I loved. I brought most of my books home every day to study. I was a conscientious student and had the grades to prove it. I was focused, and nothing was going to deter me. Yes, I was going to be a sexy beauty even though I wore an undershirt instead of a bra and carried an old, heavy briefcase with books and makeup inside.

Mom was making a change in herself too. She lost a lot of weight because of the stress. She had to get herself some new clothes. A lot of times she wanted me to go with her. She even started sending me by myself to pick out a dress for her. I was enjoying this part. I had a real eye for picking out what would look good on her. I knew what patterns, colors, and styles looked the best on Mom. I heard her tell some of the neighbor ladies once, "If my Mary had her way, I would be sitting out here on the stoop gabbing in a suit with heels."

She was right, I would have done that. I also knew she was secretly enjoying letting me dress her up.

"Chris, let's invite some guys over, ok?" Alice asked my mom as a WIBG radio station was playing in the background. The three of us were sitting at the too big for our kitchen table, drinking Pepsi. The table was the last remains of what had been Mom's beautiful dining room outfit, complete with a glassed-in front china cabinet. Mom and Alice liked to drink their Pepsi with cherry juice. I liked mine at room temperature.

19

I could tell Mom was thinking over Alice's offer of inviting some guys to come over. She already started going out with girlfriends occasionally. Alice was the youngest daughter of the woman that lived across the hall from us when dad died. She had become good friends with both of us. Alice and I liked music and dancing. Mom and Alice liked playing cards and gabbing. Mom and I seemed to get along better when Alice was around.

Life was starting to feel like it had a rhythm and normalcy to me again. There had been a bitterness growing in me that I could almost taste. With Alice in our daily lives, it took our focus off each other and added a little playfulness into the mix. It was good for all of us.

"No Alice, they would be way too young for me," Mom worried at the table.

"Chris, we'll tell them your twenty-five instead of thirty-seven. They will believe it," Alice insisted.

"Wait a minute, how can I have a daughter that is twelve going on twenty and only be twenty-five myself?" Mom quipped.

She said that because I had been caught several times with my makeup on. I looked at her thoughtfully. I pushed my chair back.

"Mom let's try something," I said.

I went and got her makeup, brushes, and hairpins from her bedroom. Alice grinned. She and I worked on her while Mom sipped her cherry-juice Pepsi with little protest. The idea was to have her look twenty-five, and for me, well, to look as young as possible. I would do it for her, just this once. By the end of it, Mom was wearing a pretty red summer dress and looked good. It would be up to the guys to decide if she looked twenty-five. Within a short time, they called to say they were on their way over.

Alice and I walked out to show them how to get to our building. They drove up in their old clunker of a car and got out. The first thing one of the guys did was walk up to me and put his arm around my waist. He said, "Hi, you must be Christine."

I blinked at him, my lips pressed into a line. Alice turned to us.

"No, that's Mary. Christine is her mother," Alice explained.

"Wait a minute, how old are you, Mary?" he asked.

"I'll be ten next month!" I answered in what I hoped sounded like a baby voice.

The guys didn't stay long that night. Nobody wondered why. But it wasn't long before Mom did find a boyfriend, all on her own. He was going to come over for dinner on Saturday. It was going to be a special dinner, and everyone was in a good mood. When Mom was in a good mood, it trickled down to each of us.

In my whole life, Mom never baked a cookie or a cake. She was a good cook. She just never baked. I knew Tom must be special because Mom was making a Boston Cream pie for dessert. It was from a box, but she was laughing like a child. She had cut one of the layers in half and it turned out perfect. It smelled perfect coming out of the oven, too.

After dinner was over, Tom gave Ed and me a ten-dollar bill. He told us to go to the corner and buy some ice cream or whatever we wanted. I made sure we were back in ten minutes. I was smarter than he thought I was.

They went out drinking frequently. I was now the official babysitter for my little brothers. Tom was spending more and more time at our house until the fateful morning he was there when we woke up. I didn't like where this was going.

I also noticed that Mom's family was never over for coffee or playing cards anymore. They argued with Tom. Aunt Lina and Theresa told Mom that something wasn't right with him.

"Christine, I think you should let him go," one of them said.

"You just don't know him like I do," Mom waved a hand at them.

She couldn't see the signs. But I could tell something wasn't right about Tom. It didn't take long for his fake niceness to us to wear off. He never officially moved in. But somehow, he was just there all the time. Unlike when Alice was around which helped my relationship with my mother, when Tom was around, we clashed like Siamese fighting fish. We wanted blood or death.

Chapter 5

What a hell of a life it was when I turned thirteen. I made friends easily enough, but I had to keep them at a distance because of my family life. I was required to be home fifteen minutes after school let out. If I hurried, that was exactly how long it took.

Most of my friends went to the corner store for sodas after school. I would never tell them I only had fifteen minutes to get home and no money to buy a soda if I did have the time. I knew I came off bratty or snobbish, but that was better than trying to explain my home life.

I would no sooner get through the front door when it would start. Not, "How was your day?" Not, "What did you learn?" No. Instead, I was greeted by a sink full of dishes that needed to be done and floors that had to be wet-moped.

My sweet mother from my childhood had been replaced by Cinderella's stepmother. I fought the injustice with the only weapon that I had. My mouth. And I used it, often and loudly to my detriment. I saw Mom sitting on the couch watching TV once. I was panting from running straight home after school. I knew I couldn't go back outside and play. Not with a mountain of dishes in the sink. Mom's eyes flicked to me.

"Are you going to start, yet? I need the big pot for dinner tonight."

I swallowed. "Can't you do the dishes? You don't have to wait for me. I've been at school all day."

"Don't get smart with me. The dishes are your job. Who else is going to cook for you?"

"Mom, I'm sick of this! What are you doing all day that you can't do it?"

No matter how hard I tried, she wouldn't let me win. She stopped letting me go outside. At first, I would get grounded for a day or a week. Then anything I did wrong earned me a month. My brothers were too young to say or do anything. They stayed out of our battles.

That June when school was out, it wasn't even two days in, and I was grounded for the summer. This was just a way to keep me under her thumb and close by. I had to grovel and beg when I couldn't stand being cooped up in the house for another minute.

Tom was worse than Mom. I believe he delighted in tormenting us. We had our favorite TV shows we liked to watch. Ed, Dave, and I would sit on the floor. Sunlight filtered through the curtains and warmed the room. We laughed at the characters on screen. Tom walked in and plopped on the couch. My brothers and I went quiet. Not even a minute passed. Tom groaned. "Change the channel to something else, would ya?"

He complained about having to watch some stupid kid show. Then he threatened to go out for some drinks until Mom changed the channel to something he wanted to watch. She always put him first. For the life of me, I could not understand why she loved him or could accept what was happening to us.

Along the way, I started perfecting a system that allowed me to be in a moment physically, but not emotionally or mentally, because getting mad only got me punished. I would sense what was happening and try and gauge the response needed for the situation. If my mother was mad about something, I did what I needed to do. I moved on autopilot. But later at night, would I let myself experience the moment and my true feelings. How mad I was for having to stay inside instead of enjoying the summer. How I felt about Mom putting Tom first instead of us. I let myself feel everything for a moment. Then I pushed all my bad feelings to the farthest part of my mind. I locked them in a closet with my heart.

I put up walls. I set up a guard, my inner little girl. The me in the mirror that told me to scream on that first, terrible day. She stood guard where all my feelings and memories were. I didn't have to face them. I didn't have to face anything when it happened. I could do whatever I sensed was needed. I was in control, as much as I could be at thirteen.

But the hardest feeling to get control over was anger. Life was tough all the time. But I managed. I watched out for my brothers. I did what I had to do to get by. I stood up for myself when no one else would. I fought hard. I fought and I fought. I could push my thoughts and feelings to the back of my mind. But leaving my anger unresolved hurt me in ways I wouldn't know until later. I wasn't aware of the mystical thread that connected what happened to me on the outside to what was happening to my heart and mind on the inside.

I had an 8th grade science teacher that was wondering if I had given any thought to going to college. I enjoyed Science more than any other class. When a question was asked, my hand would be the first one to go up. Even though college would be a long way off, I didn't have a single seed of hope about attending. Mrs. Moore asked me to come to the front after class let out one day. I approached her desk quietly.

"Mary, the report you turned in was exceptional. You have a brilliant mind for knowledge and testing ideas. You should consider studying in a scientific field someday."

Beautiful, good feelings blossomed inside me. But I pushed them to the back of my mind. I put my head down and said, "Oh. I don't know." Mrs. Moore looked concerned.

"Why not, Mary? I think you have a good shot in college."

I just shrugged, puzzled. "I'm 13."

Mrs. Moore chuckled. "Well, that's true. But I encourage you to think about it, even just a little. Let me know if you change your mind."

I nodded. Mrs. Moore dismissed me, and I quickly walked away. My heart jumped inside me for the rest of the day. I kept moving and doing what I needed to do. The rest of the day passed in a blur. Later in bed, I went go over the conversation we had. I let myself enjoy the good feeling that moment brought me. My heart blossomed again. The feeling that someone thought I could make it to college. She thought I was smart. I smiled into my pillow.

I had good moments like this. I would enjoy the feelings those moments brought me later when I was alone in my private world. A boy would tell me how pretty I was and how much he liked me. That should have warmed my heart and made me feel good the moment he said it. But at the time it was just words flowing through my brain, to be savored later when it would be safe to feel the sweetness of each word and the kindness in his eyes.

This was something my little girl must have put in place for me. Just like how I pushed the tough, bad moments of my life to the farthest back of my mind and locked them away. I pushed the good moments and feelings aside too. My inner little girl stood guard over the good and bad memories and all the feelings that came with them. When I was safe and alone at night, she unlocked the good memories, just a crack. I could feel the warmth from Mrs. Moore's encouragement. I could blush at a boy telling me he liked me. She stood guard over my memories and feelings until it was safe to feel.

Aunt Lina and Uncle Harry were still in my periphery even though they never came over to our house anymore. I didn't see my favorite aunt and uncle because Mom was still with Tom. On the one rare occasion when all of us were at Aunt Lina and Uncle Harry's house, Mom promised me I could spend the night. These became rare treats for me. But before the visit ended, Mom and Tom got into one of their usual arguments. He insisted on leaving and taking me with them. At first, Mom did stand up for me.

"Tom, I already told her she could stay."

"Well, she shouldn't be allowed to. The house was a mess when we left."

I started to cry. "Uncle Harry, please don't make me go back."

"It's up to your mom pumpkin," Uncle Harry said.

I knew he was upset because he had very fair skin and blonde hair that was so light it was almost white. But now his face was red up to his scalp. Tom had a bullet stare on Mom, just daring her to cross him. She turned to me.

"Get your coat, Mary. You're going home with us," Mom stated.

It was like shards of broken glass jammed in my heart. I couldn't stop the pain. I had already opened myself up to the happiness staying with my aunt and uncle would have brought me. There was so little happiness in my life anymore. This was more than I could bear. As I headed for the door my uncle gave me a big hug and whispered, "You know our number. If he ever touches you, call us and we will be right there to get you."

I wish they could have done something sooner.

Mom and Tom's fights were escalating. Their screaming could be heard two buildings over. They mostly fought over his drinking and going out. Mom wasn't the kind of woman that liked to drink. And there were only a few times I ever saw her tipsy. Tom was a functioning alcoholic. He started his days with a beer, and he ended his day with many beers. How he managed to do his job every day at the shipyard was beyond my understanding.

Mom was also worried about other women in his life. On one occasion she left and went to Baltimore to bring Tom back from some young girl he went off with.

"What in God's name is wrong with my mother?" I thought.

But no one had an answer for me. By now, all her family told her to drop this guy. Her answer was just to stay away from them and to let them know, in no uncertain terms, that it wasn't any of their business.

This was so embarrassing to me. And there wasn't a thing I could do to change it. I knew this was not how I wanted to live my life. I knew what a good home life felt like. I had experienced it for ten years. A loving mother and father. Surrounded by family and loved ones. Guidance, care, and happiness. Fun conversations around the dinner table. Saying prayers before bed. And most of all, a child living a child's life. I so desperately wanted that again. I was in a nightmare, and I didn't know how to wake myself up. I was starting to feel myself being sucked into this new reality that I didn't want.

This is just the way it is now, Mary. Accept it, I told myself.

But I couldn't. I was put into this new life through the choices of the people around me. By my mother, that was supposed to care for me. By my father, who left me. I would not accept this as normal. I had to keep reminding myself what normal felt like. At the base of what I wanted, was to feel loved. I needed to feel loved more than I needed food to eat. I was starving.

There was a knock on our front door. Tom's wife and children stood on the threshold. I was stunned, and so was Mom. I don't think Mom knew about them. That poor woman came to get the father of her children. Just like Mom had done when Tom was off and cheating on her with that girl from Baltimore. But Mom must have had an inkling because I overheard them talking one night, a few months back.

They were cozy in the living room. The boys had been put to bed long ago. I was sitting at the kitchen table, finishing up a report for history class. I wanted to submit my project with a typed report attached. It was slow going because the only thing I knew about typing was the alphabet. If I needed a "C" I found the letter "C" and typed it. I had no idea it was going to be so tedious to work with a typewriter. But I was committed to finishing, even if it took all night. But when I heard the word "married", my slow-moving fingers stopped abruptly. I was all ears.

"I need to know why you won't marry me, Tom. You said you wanted to wait and see how things worked out. Everything has worked out fine."

Oh God, is my mother delusional?

That's what I thought back then. Now the answer to her question was standing at our front door. Mom was not going to be able to keep this problem to herself. No more pretending to everyone that Tom was this great guy looking out for her and her children. What a laugh that was. Everyone had his number except her. I thought this would be the end of their relationship, but to my utter disbelief, it wasn't. I was never sent outside as much as I was when all of this was going on. I couldn't be in the room with the adults. Mom told me to take my brothers outside and play as if nothing was wrong. As far as they were concerned, everything was hush-hush, at least around me.

The only thing that kept me sane through all of this was not just my ability to shut pain out but my capacity to dream. I would be full of delight when I had some free time to sit out on the balcony drinking a Pepsi and listening to the radio. I would daydream in full technicolor about how my life would be when I turned eighteen. That was going to be the day I walked out the front door and never returned. I kept this dream front and center in my mind. I would be free to leave. In my dream, I would live in a pretty house, and it would be neat and tidy. Mealtime would be a special moment for talking and laughing.

I had a couple of requirements for this new life I would be living. The first one was a dishwasher. I wanted to just put the dishes inside and press a button to get them clean. Oh my, yes, I had to have one of those. I wanted to throw my hands up toward heaven just like Scarlett O'Hara did in *Gone with the Wind* and declare, "As God is my witness, I will never wash another dish!"

The second part of my dream was regarding my husband, the rock star legend Ricky Nelson. But I was only thirteen, so I had time. Between dreaming and a deep dedication for protecting my heart and mind, I was doing all right. I just wasn't aware that every time I kept myself from feeling pain, it didn't evaporate. It was taking up residency on the other side of the door to my heart. And there was only a ten-year-old little girl holding the door shut. Thank goodness she was a strong little girl.

Chapter 6

"Mary, when that TV show is over, would you come into the kitchen, please?"

Was that my mother's soft voice talking to me? The TV show could wait. I had to find out what was on her mind.

"Honey, Tom and I have a surprise for you. You're going to be getting a new baby brother or sister," Mom smiled.

My first reaction was shock. What do I say? How was I supposed to handle this new, devastating news? My voice said, "Oh, that's nice."

I knew my face had to be giving away my true thoughts. I had to get away from them now. My safe haven was the bathroom, where I excused myself to.

I shut the bathroom door and gripped the sink. How was I going to handle this news? The whole idea was disgusting to me. I was fourteen. My mother was thirty-nine. She was not married, and her boyfriend was already married to someone else.

I searched my heart. How did I feel about this? Disgust, spelled with a capital "D". But what could I say about this that wouldn't get me a slap in the face or grounded for the rest of my life?

I was in the safe room for a long time, when my little girl came up with something. Mom was old and her chances of carrying a baby full term were iffy. No, she would never have this baby. Not that I wanted anything to happen to Mom or the baby, I didn't. I just wanted the problem to go away. This was self-preservation acting. I pushed my feelings of shock and disgust to the farthest part of my mind. My little girl stood guard before the door to my heart again.

As soon as I did a pretend flush and walked out the door, I was called back into the kitchen again. The smiles were gone from Mom and Tom's faces now. "Well Mary, you didn't seem very excited about our news," Mom said patiently. "What's your problem?"

I put on a big smile for them. "No Mom, I really am happy. Wouldn't it be wonderful if you had a little girl? It would be like having a real live doll to play with. When will the baby arrive?" I asked. It was the right response my mom needed to hear.

As the months passed and Mom got bigger and bigger, she became very embarrassed by her situation. She tried to talk Tom into moving us someplace else to live. I don't think I could have survived a move away from the one friend close to my age. Patty was the only real friend that I had. She lived in the building in front of mine. If I was out on the balcony and she had her window open, we could yell back and forth to each other. Best of all, she didn't seem to mind my crazy family.

Even with braces on both of her legs because of polio, she would climb the three flights of steps to spend the day with me, which is where I was most of the time because of being grounded. No, I would go crazy if we moved away. I worried about that happening up until Mom went into labor. It was April 11, 1963. I answered our new phone that had just recently been installed.

"Hello?" I said with what I thought would be a professional-sounding voice for a fourteen-year-old.

"Mary, the baby was just born. It's a beautiful, healthy baby girl!" Tom said. I could hear the smile in his voice.

It's a girl! I felt truly happy at that moment. Nine months had passed since I was first shocked by the news that my mom was pregnant. But now, my feelings and worries morphed into something new. I had a baby sister. I wasn't the only girl in the family anymore. I couldn't believe how excited I felt about this new baby. I cheered. I jumped up and down and dropped the phone to the floor.

The new baby girl was named Donnamarie; one name, not two. I couldn't wait to get to the hospital and see her. As soon as Tom got home, I would ask him to take me shopping so she would have something special to wear home. I didn't know it, but the dress I found was a baptismal dress. Still, it looked beautiful in the store. I wanted it for her, along with a pair of rubber underpants that had ruffles all around.

For once Tom and I were on the same page. The next day, as I stood looking into the nursery at my baby sister, I couldn't believe the feeling of love and protectiveness I felt for her. I was in awe. But had I not learned my lesson? Love hurts.

Mom was not recuperating from having the baby. She didn't feel well most days. She would walk the floor holding her stomach. She cried most nights. It turned out to be cancer.

They did surgery and removed part of her stomach and colon. Mom was put on bed rest and medication to recover. I helped take care of my siblings and the house, as best as I could. I tried to take care of what mattered most. These were some dark days for all of us. Regrettably, I was about to make them even darker.

With Mom in the hospital that left Tom and me at home without Mom as a referee. We had gotten into an argument over something, and I refused to agree with him. Whether he was drunk or upset over Mom, I didn't know and didn't care. But at some point, I must have crossed over some invisible line. Because Tom back-handed me right across the face.

Tom knew instantly that he'd made one big mistake. But he didn't apologize. Our eyes were locked. There was no trace of fear on my face. I wasn't afraid of him now. The only thing that could be on my face was the contempt and hatred that I felt for this poor excuse of a man.

I waited for him to leave. I did what I had been trained to do. I dialed TI58358. Within minutes my aunt and uncle were packing me up. They told me not to worry about anything. And I didn't. I just went with them. I was safe and at peace for a few days. I don't know what happened or what was said, but I returned home later. It was only a matter of time until Mom heard about it.

I might as well get this over with, I thought, as I gave a big push to the hospital door. Mom looked pale and weak lying in bed. As she turned to look at me, I could already see the anger in her eyes.

I think brown eyes show anger and hate more fiercely than blue eyes. With the blue-eyed people in my life, their eyes still seemed to twinkle, even when they were yelling. Mom's eyes were flaring. I half expected them to turn red.

"Well, you really made a mess this time, Mary. You deliberately waited until I was in the hospital with a new baby at home to start your shit. If I had been there, I would have smacked you too. You're a damn troublemaker," She growled.

There was nothing I could say that would help me. My mind was blank. I looked at her with all the hurt I felt and walked right back out the door.

I could hear her yelling, "Get back in here!"

I would have loved to run away that day, but I was smart enough to know that never works. I don't know how much my so-called "trouble-making" had to do with it, but as soon as Mom was released from the doctor, she was making plans to move us out of Jersey to Ashland, Kentucky. Tom had a sister that lived there with an empty house next door. Evidently, Mom wanted to get us as far away from her family as possible. I would lose contact with Patty, Uncle Harry, and Aunt Lina. I wouldn't see my cousins anymore if we moved. Nothing could have prepared me for this.

Chapter 7

Of course, the move happened in July. This time there were no speeches about our missed birthday parties and no Tasty Cakes. I'm not sure there was even a card. I didn't feel like celebrating anyway. No one sent anything for Ed or my birthday. No family, and no friends. No one cared a fig about me. Maybe my little brothers cared about me, but they couldn't fill the void in my life. Nothing in my life had happiness connected to it.

I stepped inside the door to the house we would call home. It was a ramshackle old house. The front door opened into a living room. To the left of the door was a double bed that would be Tom and Mom's. There was an old couch on the other wall that did not open to a bed, but I would sleep on it every night anyway. And what room could be complete without a TV?

This room was approximately twelve by twelve. It flowed into the next room of the same dimensions that contained bunk beds for the boys and Donna's crib. Next on our tour was the coup de grace, the kitchen. This room was a little bigger, maybe fourteen by twelve. And as you looked to the other side of the kitchen, you could see an old curtain that covered an archway that went into the bathroom. There was no door to the bathroom. I had never seen anything more humiliating in my whole life. Until I walked to the other side of the curtain.

Old toilet? Check. Old claw foot tub? Check. Cracked mirror hanging on the wall with a rusty nail? Check. And the worst part was that I knew I was stuck here. This was going to be my new life. Everything an all-American family of six could want. God help me. How could I make this work?

I begged and begged to go live with my Aunt Lina and Uncle Harry in New Jersey. Not a chance in hell that was going to happen. I had never been so lonely or depressed. I could easily imagine the life that I could be living under decent circumstances. I made friends easily. I was smart. It could be fun starting a new high school and being the new girl. I wouldn't have shied away from that. To work my way into a clique. To be able to have friends over after school. To get dressed up and go to parties. Find a special boyfriend that would give me his school ring.

Oh my, yes, I would love that life.

But I wasn't dealing with ordinary circumstances. How was I going to make this work? I could easily be the laughingstock of the school if anyone found out about my home life. I had one month to figure it out. One month to the start of the new school year. This time without family, without a friend I knew.

To my surprise, Mom walked me to school that first day, probably because of papers that needed to be signed. This was the first-time Mom and I had spent any time together, just the two of us. By this time, Mom had recovered enough from having the baby, treatment, and her surgery. She was stronger again and cancer-free.

It was a fairly long walk. I know she was trying to help me adjust to these new circumstances. I was enjoying her positive focus on me. We approached the school, which was about half the size of my last school. I didn't think I would ever get out of grade school. Not because of my scores, but because they kept adding grades to the school I went to in New Jersey. When I was in seventh, they added the eighth grade. When I was in the eighth grade, they added the ninth grade. I was beginning to believe I was going to graduate high school right from the Davis Elementary building. That is, until Mom moved us away. And here we were, in Kentucky.

As we approached the high school building, you could see the different cliques. Cliques were nothing more than birds of a feather flocking together. Always on the other side of the street from a school, would be the high and mighty badasses. Several of the truly nice, welcoming girls came right up to us and introduced themselves. They asked me what grade I was in. I told them all about being in the ninth grade and still being in an elementary school, which gave them a chuckle. Finally, I managed to get to high school.

Having Mom with me on that first day helped a lot. Mom was usually focused on Tom and the new baby. And there was so much to do with the big move. So when Mom took a moment just to walk me to school on my first day, it was special to me. I was nervous and excited. I didn't want to do this alone. Mom was here when I needed her.

I'm sure there would have been a lot of high school girls that would have been embarrassed to have their mother walk them to school, but not me. I was aware of how this Norman Rockwell moment looked. She just looked like a nice mom walking her daughter to school. One of the nice, welcoming girls outside of the school smiled at my mother.

"Don't worry about Mary, Mrs. Falkenburg. We will take good care of her."

My mother smiled at her. "That warms my heart. Thank you for looking out for my Mary."

The girls waved to me as Mom and I walked to the front doors. They hoped to see me at lunch. These sweet, innocent-looking girls did not have a clue what my life was like. I wanted to be them. I had been them.

On the surface, I had everything going for me. I was pretty enough. I was a sweet person, who truly cared about people. I got along with almost everyone outside of my family. And Mother Nature had finally dropped a few curves on me. On the surface, I was a winner. But inside, I felt like crabgrass.

Crabgrass was green and looked good from a distance, but it wasn't something you wanted in your lawn. I was strong and resilient on the

35

surface. But inside my heart were bare, dry patches starving for happiness and real love. I knew I was different from other girls my age. I couldn't be like them, not with what I had been through. Not with what my life was like at home. I didn't want anyone to know. I couldn't be a flower or a healthy blade of grass like other girls.

It didn't take long before I opened the front door to find the class president at my door. George from my homeroom was standing there selling something. My eyes went wide. He looked confused. Just beyond the doorway was a messy living room. My blanket was thrown over one part of the couch. Toys were scattered on the floor. A half-empty laundry basket full of clothes sat on the coffee table. The TV blared a random show. I bet George could hear my brothers Ed and Dave in the kitchen playing with toys. I knew I left a mop and bucket leaning against one wall.

"Mary, do you live here?" George asked, as his eyes took in the bed in the living room and the ratty couch. I was humiliated beyond belief. I pulled out a fake laugh.

"No, I'm just babysitting. I live up the street, but no one is home right now. You don't need to stop by," I said.

I pointed to a pretty white house up the street. George glanced, but I could see the gears turning in his mind. I'm sure he didn't buy it; I wasn't that good of an actress. And if it wasn't bad enough having one drunk, my mother's mean, alcoholic, father had come to stay with us. He was so mean to my brothers that it scared me.

My brother Ed's teacher contacted Mom about him telling "lies" at school. I don't know if what he was telling them was a lie or not. If it was a lie, I know he was just trying to protect himself at eleven. More than likely, it was the truth about what was going on with us at home. But no one wanted to believe it. Especially not my mother.

A few months after moving in, I noticed a change in Tom. He started complimenting me on how clean I was keeping the kitchen and bathroom. I couldn't believe how nice he was treating me. This was a new side to him. He was nice and friendly for a few weeks. He even gave me some extra money, so I could go with the girls and have a Pepsi after school. Things were really starting to improve.

Then one Saturday, I was standing at the kitchen sink washing lunch dishes. Mom was next door visiting Tom's sister. Everyone was gone but Tom and me. I was just finishing up the dishes when Tom walked up behind me. He put his face near my neck and brought both arms around. He started groping my breasts. I whipped around and shoved him away.

"What do you think you're doing? I'm telling Mom as soon as she walks through that door!" I yelled.

Tom didn't say a word. But he left. I wasn't scared. I was pissed off. As soon as Mom walked in, I blasted into her.

"Just ask him, just ask him what he did," I said with all the strength in my voice, but without yelling at her.

I told her exactly what happened. She was as angry as I have even seen her. When Tom came back, she lit into him as soon as he walked in the door. He talked her into going down to the river to talk. I know she believed me when I told her, so I don't know how he ever explained it away. All Mom said to me later that day was, "People make mistakes. He had been drinking. But you will never have to worry about it happening again, Mary."

How do you say something like that to your daughter? She forgave him! That betrayal from my mother was harder to accept than Tom molesting me. After that, I didn't care what I did. I didn't care what lies I told. I would sneak out in the middle of the night, to party.

"You want to come to my house and see me? Well come on over," I told my friends at school. What the hell did I care? All the dynamics changed after that incident in the kitchen. It was sort of a truce. I stayed out of their way, and they stayed out of mine.

Chapter 8

When June rolled around a year later, Mom made an announcement. We were moving again. This time the move would take us to Toledo, Ohio. Tom had found a good job and a nice place for us to live.

"No, Mom. I don't want to move again. Why do you keep doing this to us?" I groaned.

Mom sighed. She didn't get angry at my honesty towards her announcement. "I'm sorry but it's better for me," Mom answered. "I can't take care of you and the others on my own."

And I knew she thought it was true. But I disagreed. I looked off to the side. I stared at a sunbeam through the kitchen window, biting my lip.

Mom and I grew much closer since Tom's visit to Toledo. He left to find a new job and continue to provide for us, instead of being at the house in Kentucky. With Tom out of town, Mom was more honest with me. We had some heart-to-heart conversations over the last few months. Mom told me how afraid she was that we would be taken away from her because she wasn't able to take care of us. The checks from the SSA helped all of us financially, but in Mom's mind life wasn't the same since my father passed away.

But everything as it was now, was fine to her. I believe that was the story she told herself so she could accept the choices she had made. I listened. I reassured her that she was still my mom. But Mom couldn't shake that her worries were the absolute truth. She gave me a wistful smile. I knew my assurances were appreciated somewhere in her heart.

We started talking, not screaming, at each other because of our conversations. I also believe she wanted to calm me down, for fear I would tell someone what happened between me and Tom. I probably would have, if my aunt and uncle were still in my life. But we didn't have a phone, and I had not heard from them the whole time we were in Kentucky. I never reported Tom about the incident. Mom's voice pulled me away from my thoughts.

"Mary, I think this is really going to be better. Let's go, and if you're not happy you can go back to New Jersey and live with Aunt Lina and Uncle Harry, I promise."

I frowned thoughtfully. That was a tempting offer. Even after all this time, I knew I would be welcomed with open arms. In my whole life, I never went to bed without praying for my Watson family. Their memory was the one thing I held onto tightly. I loved them and I knew they loved me. The memories I have of Aunt Lina and Uncle Harry were my prized possession.

They were the one good thing no one could change, my lifeline to happiness. Just the thought of them and my cousins always made me feel better. The times I ate dinner over at their house, surrounded by laughs and happy conversations. The moments Barbara Ann taught me how to apply lipstick and roll my hair. The earlier times I ran outside under the blue sky and caught pretend bad guys with my cousins Skip and Eddie.

Sometimes that was all I had to keep me going. My happy memories of the Watson family and my inner little girl's protection during the ugly moments of my day. I filtered every feeling and thought to the back of my mind. After five years, I was beginning to have some insight into what was happening to me inside my mind and heart. Before daddy died, the situations around me, were one with me. Something happened, and I naturally reacted to it.

Now, as bad as everything was in the present, I was able to process what I could do about these moments in a very unconnected way. Moving here to Kentucky and not knowing anyone. Giving up everyone I loved or even knew. Faced with this year of unknowns, my inner little girl had been there for me. I could deal with this moving again change too. I just had to convince myself I could do it.

I went to the bathroom and splashed cold water on my face. I looked at myself in the broken mirror hanging by a rusty nail. I remembered being in this exact same spot the Saturday before my first day of high school.

"OK Mary, you're stuck in this little shack. You don't know anyone, and if you did you probably wouldn't be allowed to go see them anyway. So, what can we do to get ready for this?" I had asked myself in the mirror then. I remembered that there wasn't a cloud in the sky.

"Well, there is that beautiful, bright sun. Get a blanket and get a tan. That will help you look better for the first day of school, when you get to meet everyone," I told myself.

And I did just that. The sun warmed my skin, and my nervousness melted away. When Mom walked me to school on the first day, I knew I looked my best. I could hold my chin up high. But that wasn't all I could do to make the best of the year in Kentucky.

"See if you can get some babysitting jobs and earn a little money to buy some pretty new clothes for school," I said to myself while walking home one day. There were plenty of small families and nice houses. I could make this work.

"Don't worry we can make this work," I promised myself while I mopped the floor at home.

"Look what a pretty picture you're creating with your mom, standing in the schoolyard together, looking as if the two of you were so close you didn't want to part," I thought when the welcoming group of girls spotted us. To anyone else, I could make my excuses. I could smile and be friendly to everyone that met me.

"No, I can't go to your house to study with you. I'm so sorry but my mom likes me at home with her. My dad is away a lot and I have to help with our new baby. Oh, Didn't I tell you? I have a beautiful baby sister that was born last year!"

I knew how to make the right face and say the right thing I needed to, just get by. I hoped to God no one ever found out the truth.

"What's my address?"

"Oh, I'm sorry, I'm not allowed to give that out. My parents are so protective of our privacy."

My inner little girl helped me with every single idea I needed to weather these moments in my life. With her protection, the system I had in place in my mind allowed me to make it through some hellish situations with as little pain as possible. It was not like I had an imaginary friend that came to my rescue. She was the new Mary, and I could watch her work through the uncertainties of life. I shoved all the pain I couldn't face to the farthest part of my mind. I didn't want to ask myself why all of this was happening to me. The question would have sucked me in, and never let me go.

I read somewhere from a book years later, that trying to figure out life as it is happening would be like a fish trying to understand the water it lived in. Water had always been a part of its life. Unless the fish is scooped up outside of the water, how could it recognize what water is? How could I understand what was happening in my life at the time and why, when it was the home environment I was stuck in? What I was doing was learning to cope in the only way I knew how. I was learning to analyze my situations and feelings from a new perspective.

Of course, the month we moved again was around the first of July, in 1965. It was a bright beautiful day when all of us got off the bus in Toledo, Ohio. Tom was there to meet us as promised. He had booked us into a downtown hotel because our house wouldn't be available to move into until the next day.

We had dinner in a little restaurant and went up to our room. For some reason they wanted me to go back to the restaurant. I think something had been left behind. Well, I got lost so it took some extra time for me to find the place on the way back. It was getting dark, but the air was still warm. I walked alone, occasionally glancing around to get my bearings. Donna's pacifier was tucked in my pocket from the restaurant. A man walked in my way from a nearby convenience store. I stopped and stared at him.

"You look lost, honey. Need a hand?" he asked.

"No, I'm all right. Thank you," I answered.

The man laughed, a broad smile on his face. "Oh, we got a southern belle here," he commented.

I kept my expression carefully blank. *No, I'm not from the south*, I thought.

"Thanks," I said flatly.

I ducked into a nearby awning for another restaurant. I sought refuge in the bathroom. I left the restaurant later with a steady breath. It was pitch black outside now. I glanced over my shoulder. No one followed me, thank goodness.

By the time I got back, my mother was in tears. She realized what she had done. She had sent her teenage daughter out in a strange city by herself, who probably didn't even know how to get back. When I got back to our room, Mom pulled me into the biggest hug she had ever given me since I was a little girl. She held my face in her hands. Tears streamed down her face.

"Mary, oh Mary. Thank God you're okay! I'm so, so sorry," Mom sobbed.

I was stunned. I patted her back. Mom told me she had never been so scared in her life and so happy to see my face now. I could feel that what she was saying was the truth. It felt amazing. I held her back tight. I buried my face in her neck. Mom's tears soaked into my top. At this moment, it was the most love I had felt from my mother in years. *Maybe it will be different here in Toledo.*

Chapter 9

Tom drove us to the house the next day. It was a palace compared to the place we had lived in. It had beautiful hardwood floors with lots of windows. The house looked out across the street to a well-attended park with a big pool.

Oh, the kids are going to love that, I thought. I planned to take Dave and Ed to the pool the first chance I could.

We didn't have any furniture so we were buying all new stuff, thank goodness. We didn't even care that we didn't have any beds. We all picked out a spot on the floor and declared it our space.

We walked over to the park for a while and checked everything out. There was a little hamburger place not far away. We waited and waited, and no one came over to take our order. Finally, I looked up and read the sign that said, "Place orders at the counter". *Duh*, I thought. Tom slapped his forehead. Mom gasped. Mom, Tom, Dave, Ed, and I all started laughing at the same time. Donnamarie babbled along with us. These were the kind of times I had dreamed about. There were smiles on all our faces as we walked home, with full bellies and laughter in our hearts.

I took the baby and made a spot for her next to me so we could cuddle that night. Donnamarie did not work as a name. I know Mom thought that was the most beautiful name she had ever heard, but no one used it. Not even Mom. So we called her Donna for short. I loved that little baby with my whole heart. She was beautiful and a good baby. I would be sixteen in a few weeks. Ed would be twelve, and Dave ten. Donna would be two. Things were going so well I could hardly believe it.

The next day we went shopping for new furniture. Tom and Mom took us with them. To my amazement, they agreed with some of the things that I liked for the house. In 1965 everyone was into greens, oranges, and earth tones. I knew because I read every magazine I could get my hands on, in the stores or from the library. Reading had always been my number one love.

I picked out a black sleeper sofa. I knew I would end up on the couch once again. Mom and Tom had a bedroom that contained Donna's crib. The other bedroom contained bunk beds for the boys and a bed for me. Either they thought I would be out the door shortly or Donna was going to stay in her crib forever. A sleeper sofa would help in that situation. I already planned on sleeping on the sofa and bringing Donna out of Mom's room to sleep with me. She shouldn't be in there, I knew. Tom did like his new job at the shipyard. He was making good money.

"Mary, do you remember how to get to the grocery store that we stopped at the other day?" Mom asked one day.

"I think I could find it, what do you need?" I answered.

She handed me a list and dug into her purse to fish for cash. I ducked out of the house to go shopping. It's no wonder I had no sense of direction. My mother had taught all of us that north was always in front of you. Those were the exact words she used. I was lucky I made it home safe the first night we were in Toledo.

Of course, I had since learned the hard way and with a lot of laughter from other kids that I did not have my own north. Nor did I learn to look for landmarks along the way. The outcome was inevitable, on that very fateful summer day. On the way home, I turned down the wrong street. When was I going to learn that I had no sense of direction?

I made it to the grocery store with no problem, but I was one street off on my return home. It seemed like I had been walking forever with a full bag of groceries. Suddenly, this beautiful, burgundy convertible stopped next to me. A good-looking guy asked me if I was lost.

"I'm trying to get home," I admitted.

He smiled politely. "Well, hop in. I'll help you find your house."

Oh no, I wasn't falling for that line. He did seem genuinely nice, but I wasn't getting in that car. I started walking again.

"Please wait," the gentleman said.

He got out of the car and introduced himself on the sidewalk. He said his name was Rusty. I nodded.

"What's around your house?" he asked.

I hummed. The brown paper bag shifted out of my fingers. I hiked it up. My arms were getting tired. It just had to be July.

"My house looks across a swimming pool and a park," I said. The bag started slipping down again.

"Here, let me take that. You're only a few blocks away from your house. Hop in," Rusty said.

"Really?" I asked. It was hard to believe.

Rusty laughed, and it was a beautiful sound. "Yeah, your backyard and my friend's backyard connect."

"What are the chances of that?" I said.

He smiled back. Rusty opened the passenger door for me. I gingerly gave him my groceries. He set them on the floor of the back seat. We got in his car. The engine purred to life.

"What's your name?" he asked.

"Mary," I shook his hand. His hand was bigger than mine but very warm.

I saw Rusty a lot after that. It seemed like rusty was in his friend's backyard every evening. But I liked this. Eventually, Rusty got up the nerve to ask me out. I was just happy to have someone to talk to from my yard. I had to tell him that I was sure the answer would be no.

"I doubt my mom is going to say yes," I smirked.

"Well, why don't you let me ask her?" he shrugged.

I was in such a happy place that I didn't want to do anything that might change this new family dynamic we were currently experiencing, with a new house, a new school year coming soon, and everything else.

"Sure, you can ask her, but I have a feeling the answer is going to be no," I said.

To my delight and surprise, that did not deter him. I was going to be sixteen at the end of this month. I had a feeling he was much older than I was. *Oh boy, I have a feeling this might really set her off,* I thought.

Rusty came over and introduced himself. This was the first time I didn't have to be embarrassed to have someone see where I lived. He seemed to be very comfortable around Mom. I could tell she was impressed with him. He was what my Uncle Harry would call, "A man of substance."

"If it's ok with you Mrs. Falkenburg, I would like to take Mary to the Drive-In on Saturday night," Rusty asked.

Is he crazy? I thought frantically. He could have started with hamburgers at the Yum Yum down the street, or something simple like a walk in the park. I knew this was going to come to a screeching halt.

"Sure, I don't have a problem with that Rusty," Mom said with a charming smile.

I blinked, surprised. My jaw almost dropped to the floor. What just happened here? A normal conversation between my mother and this 20-year-old guy that wanted to date me? But Mom said yes! By the time I walked him to the door I was floating.

"Thank you, Jesus," I whispered to myself.

This was one of the best days of my life. A good, normal teenage life was going to develop, thanks to this wonderful guy I already truly respected. Rusty Bilger was perfect. He had such a great laugh. His laugh made other people laugh. He was well-liked and had dozens of good friends. We instantly hit it off.

He had a job at a manufacturing company when we first met. Within a few dates, he told me he had signed up for the National Guard. He would be leaving for basic training in September. When I heard this, I felt crushed. I was already enjoying going out with this guy. It was a dream come true for me. It was made a whole lot easier by my mother and Rusty getting along so well. By the end of July, I was in love with Rusty. I couldn't imagine my life without him.

46

We started dating every night. We got along like we had always known each other. He introduced me to his very funny father and his sweet mother. I adored them both immediately. He had a younger brother named Bill that was my exact age. To me, they represented the all-American family. I spent a lot of time with them. They lived in a small but charming house that his mother decorated beautifully. And the best part? Rusty was in love with me too. It was as if we had been waiting for each other. Our relationship wasn't magical, it was better than that. It felt inevitable.

We knew this was something special. We went slow and really got to know each other. Now he was leaving in September for the service. I would be starting my junior year of high school. By the end of August, I was dreading the arrival of September, the month I always felt was the most beautiful month of the year. God always painted a different picture outside my window every day with the constant changing colors. I loved it and appreciated it. This September was different. Not only was Rusty leaving, but I found myself in a horrific situation of my own making. I realized I had not had a period in July or August.

No, please don't let this be true, I thought. Nervousness churned in my belly. I thought I was going to be sick. As if on cue, I started throwing up in the bathroom. Dread and sadness filled me. I couldn't push this away. It was too real and present to be a lie or something I could hide. It was true. My wild days in Kentucky several weeks ago were coming back to haunt me. What was I going to do? How could I come up with the words to tell Mom or Rusty?

Chapter 10

First, I had to tell her that the baby couldn't possibly be Rusty's. But when, and how? I couldn't think clearly. Rusty was getting ready to leave town and I wasn't sure of anything. The last night he was home I told him there was something I needed to tell him. It was during one of our dates. The two of us had been driving around while hanging out. Rusty turned to me.

"What is it?" he asked.

My face crumpled. I was crying so hard; I tried but I couldn't form complete sentences. This went on for a while. Rusty gently patted my back.

"Hey, whatever it is, I won't be mad at you. If you have to let me go, I—well, that hurts, but I get it," Rusty said.

Oh, Rusty, I thought. I searched his face through my tears. He thought I didn't want to wait for him to get back from the service.

"That's not—I mean, I am going to miss you. It's just—" I tried again.

"Ssh. It's going to be okay," Rusty soothed.

48

This wonderful man told me not to worry about whatever I was trying to say. He said we could write to each other while he was away and wait to see what happened. Kinder words were never so lovingly received.

The truth was, I couldn't bear the thought of losing him. Rusty was everything I had ever wanted. I loved him with my whole heart, but I couldn't see a way through this. I was pregnant, sixteen, and alone.

Just when life felt so positive and good, it felt as if a cruel joke was being played on me. I sat on our front porch steps a few days later. I played every scenario over again in my head. If I told Mom, she would want to take me back to Kentucky and make that boy marry me. No, I wouldn't do that. Get rid of the baby? No, that wasn't an option either. Have the baby and raise it myself? No, I wasn't ready for that. There was no answer for me.

Suddenly, a car whizzed by on the street out front. It had been speeding. I thought, *"If I had been in front of it, my problem would be gone."*

I had my answer. I waited. As I looked far down Summit Street, I saw a big truck coming. I was willing myself to "just keep walking". And I did. The world was very quiet. I put one foot in front of the other. My mind was quiet with only one thought: *"Just put one foot in front of the other until you get to the other side. And pray for forgiveness."*

With a heavy, beating heart, I stood up. The warm sun was on my face. The fall trees dazzled in their beautiful splendor. I didn't stop walking until I was on the side of the oncoming truck. Tires screeched. A horn blared. I was almost to the truck. Just one more step and I would be in front of it.

No, I can't do this. I jumped back as the truck was passing. I could see the terror in that driver's eyes. My eyes were identical.

The truck kept going. As best I could, I made it back to the house and into the bathroom. I couldn't stop throwing up.

"Oh God, please help me," I cried.

I sobbed as long as I needed to. I was still shaking even after I stopped. I flushed the toilet. I washed my face and took in deep breaths. When most of the shaking stopped, I left my safe room.

Mom and Tom were waiting for me. I caught them talking seriously in low murmurs. Mom looked into my eyes. Her face was tight with anxiety. She stepped toward me.

"Mary, we saw what happened," she said.

She knew what I tried to do. I don't know how she knew. I didn't even know what I was going to do until the moment I stopped.

"What were you thinking?" Tom asked.

I shook my head, arms crossed across my chest. "I tried to," I stammered.

"…Walk in front of a speeding truck?" Tom finished, incredulous.

Mom held up a finger to him. Her eyes flicked to me. I was starting to shake again. Mom could see it. Tom could see it.

"Mary, what's going on?" Mom asked.

"I'm pregnant," I whispered, horrified.

The truth tumbled out of my mouth. I told her it wasn't Rusty's. Of course, Mom started talking about tracking this boy down in Kentucky and making him marry me. But I couldn't. That wasn't the solution, not for me. I was scared and shaking and couldn't stop crying.

I admitted what I had tried to do. I finally told her I was pregnant. I felt so drained, I couldn't even think anymore. Mom let it go. She got me a glass of water and lead me to the couch. I took small, shaking sips. I laid down and slept most of the day.

When I woke up, Mom and Tom were drinking coffee in the dining room. I joined them with a cup of tea. They were very quiet.

"Mary, honey, I'm worried about you. We were thinking, maybe it would help if you went to stay with Aunt Lina and Uncle Harry. Would you like that?" she asked me quietly.

My eyes watered. This was a real lifeline. No matter what my problems were, I could work them out if I was with them. I couldn't get the "Thank you," and "Yes" out of my mouth coherently. I was sobbing again. This was my answer. My mother, who loved me through her faults and worries, was the one that provided it for me.

Mom reached out to Aunt Lina and Uncle Harry. Thank God they kept the same number, TI58358. We didn't have a phone in the house in Kentucky, but we did in Toledo. Within a week, I'd stepped off the plane in a familiar city with my packed suitcase. My aunt and uncle opened their arms, their hearts, and their home to me, just like I knew they would. They bought a new house since the last time I was in New

Jersey. This house was charming, but I loved their old place, which contained so many good memories.

It took us several days to get caught up on all the changes that had happened to all of us. Aunt Lina and Uncle Harry were so supportive of me. All they wanted to know was what I wanted to do. I told them I was certain that the best thing would be to give the baby up for adoption. The next day they started making the necessary calls.

Within a week, they had me seen by a doctor at the free clinic in the area. I was grateful for this clinic. I was only too aware of how hard I could have it, if not for places that helped girls in my situation. They never made me feel judged either, which surprised me.

I didn't have school, and I didn't want any of my old friends to see me. But I couldn't just sit around in front of the TV or help out with chores all day. To help pass the time, Uncle Harry had me help him paint a mural on one of the walls in the basement. We would work on that a little each day.

My mother sent them money to help take care of me. The kind social worker assigned to my case brought over a bag of maternity clothes as my pregnancy went on. Aunt Lina and I dug through the clothes in my bedroom. I stood before the long mirror, turning this way and that. I frowned. I was getting *huge*. Aunt Lina smiled at me in a reassuring way.

"You know Mary, with baggy clothes on, you barely look pregnant."

I had to laugh because I felt like a cow. I was now in my third trimester.

"What did the doctor say at your last visit?" Aunt Lina asked me as she sipped her coffee in her pretty kitchen.

"They said everything is fine, but I never get the same doctor twice," I said.

That was one of the drawbacks of going to a clinic. They did take care of all the paperwork for the adoption though.

"I'm healthy with no problems, but they will start seeing me once a week, starting next month," I added.

The free clinic was a lifeline for us. A hospital would have been too expensive. But the people at the free clinic only wanted to help me through this situation. They were extremely caring. And I was extremely grateful for the care and compassion I was getting from Aunt Lina and Uncle Harry too. Having my own room should have felt like heaven, but the truth was, I missed my little sister and the boys.

I called my family when I could just to hear their voices. I found out that the newness of the move to Toledo had started to wear off. Mom and Tom's relationship was back to their old habits of fighting. Aunt Lina told me after one of her telephone calls. I was really worried about all of them.

Rusty and I still corresponded by letter and occasionally by phone calls. I never did find the words to tell him why I was here in New Jersey. He had known that I always had the option of returning to New Jersey to live. He was too good a guy to bring into my chaos. I wouldn't do that to him.

When I decided to have the baby and place it for adoption, I imagined a well-established couple that wanted children, ecstatic over the idea of finally having a child of their own. I found a lot of comfort in that thought. That thought carried me through those very long months of waiting. But I was not prepared for giving birth.

Nothing was ever explained to me about what I would go through. I wasn't told how things would progress. How to prepare for and handle giving birth wasn't something that was usually talked about in the 1960s. The only thing I was told was to prepare myself for some excruciating pains, and not to come to the hospital too soon.

Chapter 11

The night I went into labor, I was terrified. At first, I thought it was just bad cramps. It felt like someone stabbed me slowly with a kitchen knife, pressing deeper and deeper into my flesh. Sharp pain flared from my belly to my lower spine. I felt a second knife, then a third, and a fourth. And that was just after a few pains.

I went to the hospital, but they said my water hadn't broken. They were going to send me home. But right after the exam, as I stood up to get dressed, water started running down my leg. I was so naïve that I didn't know that was what they were talking about. I left the clinic.

We no sooner arrived home than the real pains started. The stabs of pain were sharper. Pressure built inside of me, and it burned. I tried to breathe through the pain. I was heating up, and I didn't know why. I tried to remember if I ate anything that my body disagreed with earlier, but nothing came to mind.

"Mary are you sure you're ok? You look so white," Aunt Lina asked.

My voice shook. "Yes, it's just these pains are much worse than when I was at the hospital. But they told me not to be in any hurry to come back." I leaned against the wall. I grimaced as another sharp pain hit me.

"Let's go back anyway," Uncle Harry said, with deep concern showing on his face.

Thank goodness it was a different nurse that helped me. She told us she was going to admit me. Aunt Lina and Uncle Harry had to leave me because Skip and Ed were home alone. Barbara Ann wasn't home to watch them.

I was already having pains beyond anything I had ever experienced in my life. Sweat broke out on my skin. The clinic room wasn't cold enough to keep me cool. And the pain wouldn't stop. I was scared, and I was by myself. I squeezed my eyes tight.

Fear, like I had never experienced, set in. My mind couldn't handle it. I went to this very scary, dark place in my mind. It was pitch black. Nothing was growing under my feet. It was solid, cold rock. There was no one around me; no animals or sounds of life.

"Help!" I cried.

My voice echoed. Cold fear gripped me by the throat and wouldn't let go. I couldn't scream. I couldn't move. Every time I would try to hold onto a thought it would fade away. Until there was nothing. I realized this was a place I had never been to. A place where nothing existed, except for my consciousness.

Nothing.

Yes, only me and this one thought exists. Nothing else. The last time I thought of "nothing" as a refuge was when I was alone on a couch in Mrs. Cyr's apartment. I was left alone while the police investigated my father's passing on that horrible December morning. Nothingness gave me a moment to just be. I stayed still in this space. I tried to breathe, and just be.

But fear and pain locked me in. I couldn't escape the reality of what I was going through. I was in the height of labor, and I couldn't push any of it away to the back of my mind. The system in my mind I built up to protect me failed. *I can't do this. I can't have this baby. I'm alone. It hurts, it burns. I'm going to die.*

I gritted my teeth. *Fight Mary, this isn't right! These thoughts are wrong!*

Oh God, please help me, I begged.

Yes, that's right! God exists!

I wasn't alone. I could do this. I could survive this horrible pain and fear. I let out a powerful scream and pushed with all my might.

"Mary, Mary, can you hear me?"

I heard a faint voice. I tried to open my eyes.

"It's all over with. The baby is here and is healthy and doing fine," The nurse told me. I could hear her more clearly now.

"Is it a boy or a girl?" I asked hoarsely.

"Mary, it's better if you don't know. It will make it easier for the adoption."

I must have fallen back to sleep because two new nurses were standing around my bed. I wasn't awake enough to know if it was me they were talking about, but the words I heard were "psychotic break". I didn't know what that meant, but I did remember that nightmare I had, where I was in my hell, then nothingness. God came and saved me. I never questioned it. No one on the staff ever said a word about what a "psychotic break" meant to me.

There is no doubt in my mind that whatever strength I learned from my little inner girl, helped pull me through that harrowing experience. My little girl could and would protect me through anything. She was a part of God. She was a part of me. I knew that with unwavering, certainty.

The next morning, one of the nurses came by to check my vitals. She told me what a beautiful baby girl I had.

"I had a girl?" I asked.

"What, you didn't know?" the nurse answered.

"No, they said I shouldn't know because of the adoption."

"Well, she is beautiful. Would you like to see her?"

"Oh my, yes, please!" I couldn't believe this was happening.

As she put the tightly wrapped little bundle in my arms, all I could say was, "Thank you, thank you." When they first admitted me and I was at the beginning of my labor, they asked what name I wanted to use if the baby was a girl.

"Christine, after my mother," I said.

It never crossed my mind to name the baby anything else if it was a girl. More than anything, I wished she could be with me. She had to stay home and take care of the kids in Toledo.

"And what if it's a boy?" They asked me.

"Donald," I said. I didn't tell them the reason why, but I knew that was Rusty's real name.

I was looking down into baby Christine's beautiful eyes. I looked so hard because I wanted to remember every little detail. She didn't have much hair. Her skin was plump and pinkish. She was quiet and warm in my arms. Her eyes gently opened. They were a beautiful green shade, like soft grass on a spring day. I smiled at her. This look would have to last me a lifetime. Just that fast, the nurse took her out of my arms.

Maybe, that first nurse was correct. Because I knew, it was going to make it harder to let go of her. But I didn't doubt that I made the right choice. A kind, elderly woman that was my social worker had taken a liking to me. One day, as she was driving me back home, she confided to me that one of the doctors was going to try and adopt the baby. She didn't give me any other details, but she thought it might help me to know that, and it did. My prayer was to have a loving, established couple adopt the baby. I couldn't thank her enough for sharing that information with me, because I knew she wasn't supposed to.

I walked out of the hospital a few days later with my aunt beside me. I couldn't believe what I had gone through to get to this point. I didn't know what I wanted to do now. My aunt and uncle made it very clear that I did not have to return to my mother in Toledo, Ohio. They would have fought her this time. I knew they were sorry they had returned me the last time. But legally they didn't have a choice.

As tempting as it was to stay with them, and as crazy as it sounds, I missed everyone. Well, not Tom. I still had no use for him. But it worried me that my brothers and little sister were still stuck with him. It felt as if I had been rescued from a burning building, but the little ones were still inside. I had to go home.

Chapter 12

Things were much better than I thought they would be when I went back to Toledo two months after giving birth in New Jersey. Mom grinned when she saw me. She gave me a big hug and looked me over.

"Wow, Mary you look really good!"

She said she couldn't believe how good I looked. I smiled on the front steps. When my brother Dave saw me as I came through the door, well, I will go to the grave remembering that loving smile on his face. He was thirteen and almost as tall as me now. Ed wasn't there when I came back. I heard he was busy with his buddies and gone a lot, a teenager growing into his own life.

Donna was still a tiny little thing at four years old. I bent down to give her the biggest hug I could. She made pictures for me and told me how much she loved me. She was my baby again. She could make me smile just by walking into the room.

Mom and Tom's arguing had calmed way down. They were getting along quite well. I wondered what had caused this change in the magic duo. I learned that they had made friends with several other couples.

Tom still had his job at the shipyard and worked every day. Tom and I were civil to each other and mostly stayed out of each other's way.

His drinking was the thing that worried me. I knew he was a mean drunk. I wanted to believe things had changed, but I had an apprehension that only past experience could produce. It felt like the calm before a storm. It took about six weeks for the true Tom to show his miserable, drunken self.

We were all sitting down for one of Mom's pot roast dinners. She made them with baby carrots, little potatoes, and lots of brown gravy. One of my favorites. Mom was sitting at one end of the table and Tom was at the other. Donna sat on Tom's right, and I sat on his left. Donna started crying. She didn't want to eat. Tom's voice kept getting louder and louder over her crying. He was yelling at her until he finally told her that if she didn't shut up, she was going to get a beating.

I glanced at Mom. She had her head down, completely focused on the food. Dave sat on the other side. He ate a forkful of pot roast silently. I could see the fear in his eyes. Donna was still crying. I waited for Mom to do something. I realized that wasn't going to happen. I knew what had to be done. When I heard the word "beating" it was like a bell ringing for two fighters to step into the ring. I would have loved to rake my nails straight down Tom's face until I could see blood streaming down.

I took my chair and placed it between him and Donna. I picked up a baby carrot with her fork. I gave Donna a big smile and cooed at her like a bird. Donna immediately sniffed and paid attention to me.

"Hey little girl, are you feeling a little coo-coo today?" I chirped at her.

Donna giggled. I fluttered my lips and pretended the baby carrot was on a swing. I swung the fork toward her little mouth. Donna bit the carrot in between giggles. I praised her with a happy little chirp and wiggled in my seat. Donna enjoyed the game. I did funny things until her plate was cleared. Tom ignored us both, focused on his food in grumbling silence. I could feel the relief in Dave and Mom from where I sat.

This poor excuse of a man was never going to hurt my family again. It was lucky for Tom that Donna did eat her dinner that day. He didn't know it, but he had met his match. If he so much as touched anyone I cared about, I would fight back. He would have found out how much I was willing to fight for my family's peace. I would call the police, social services, whatever it took. He was done being the bully of this family. I had done some serious growing up while I was away. I had enough.

There is a picture of Rusty and me standing in front of my house on Easter morning. We were on our way to church for Easter service. Mom was taking pictures. Rusty had bought me a corsage for my new yellow Easter coat. She looked as happy as Rusty and I felt.

Rusty was back from the service in the National Guard. I was home from my personal war. We were just happy to be back together. We never talked about the night before he left, when I couldn't tell him what was happening with me. I had put everything behind me, just where I had put my father, my grandparents, and every other soul-wrenching, unimaginable hurt.

Rusty and I dated every day that year. There was some talk about getting married in the future. I could see that happening. That year for Christmas Mom bought me a hope chest. I started filling immediately with little gifts for myself for after I was married to Rusty.

I had a job at the Board of Education, through the "In School Work Program". I left school in my senior year to have baby Christine, so I couldn't graduate. But I was able to work. I was saving almost all the money I earned. Rusty was starting as an apprentice for the Plumbers and Steamfitter's union.

I had several friends that I hung out with from high school. I kept in touch with them, but when you have things you don't want to share, it makes bonding almost impossible. I could not form deep and true friendships with these ladies. I could never have shared my life experiences with any of them. I was too embarrassed, and I knew they could never understand. Not only that, but I had pushed my experiences so deep down inside, that I didn't face them. I never mentioned a word about my father's death, my childhood, or giving a baby up for adoption. It would hurt too much. Never, never would I share such things with my friends from school.

"Mom!" I screamed as I ran into the house. Whenever I get excited, I sound like Mini Mouse. So, she knew something was up. I had my hand stuck out with my ring finger moving up and down.

"I'm engaged, we're getting married!" I said.

"I always wanted you to marry Rusty. This makes me so happy!" Mom squealed. She hugged me around the shoulders.

I saw tears of joy in her eyes. Even Tom congratulated us with a smile. I don't think I was ever this happy. Rusty had given me the ring for my eighteenth birthday present. Somehow, from the moment Mom had met Rusty, she instinctively knew he was the one. There was never a doubt that this was meant to be. My imagination went into overdrive with all the possibilities of my wedding to Rusty.

There would be a church full of people watching as I would float down the aisle in my beautiful gown. My shoes would be made of satin with Tiffany blue bottoms. A girl has to have something blue. My hair would be swept away from my face so only the silk of the veil would be against my skin. My maid of honor and half a dozen bride maids would be in the front of the church waiting for me to arrive. My little sister would be my flower girl. Donna would spread rose petals before me as her white gown made her appear as a bride too. My eyes would look up. They would lock on Rusty, and I would see the love and desire for me in his eyes.

My imagination motor was shifted into high gear, but a reality check came during my wedding plans. I felt these signs in my body before. I gasped.

A baby? No, I can't have a baby. Not now, I thought.

The idea that I was pregnant would ruin my wonderful imagination about my perfect wedding.

Later, much later, I determined. I would focus on that after the wedding. I was excited about having Rusty's baby, but a little scared also. But it would work out somehow; I knew it would. And Rusty felt the same way when I told him. He was scared but happy. We had not set a wedding date, so we could just tell everyone that we wanted to be married in the fall.

We were married on Thanksgiving weekend, November 25, 1967. It was an extremely cold day, but the sun did shine on the bride. Rusty had graduated from St. Michael's elementary school. He had performed the duties of an altar boy and attended church every day. We had spent the last month going to the rectory for me to become a Catholic. I had no problem changing from a Methodist to a Catholic so Rusty could be married in his church.

I had been baptized a Methodist within weeks of being born. To me, it didn't matter what proper noun was attached to a religion, so long as God was at the helm. I had a very close attachment with Jesus. He had always been the one that I turned to. There were many days in my younger life that I held out my hand for him to touch me, so I would know I wasn't all alone. And each time, I felt his presence.

The church wasn't overflowing with people as I had pictured it in my imagination, but there were enough people that Mom declared, "This is a very, very, nice turnout, Mary."

I had decided on a noon service so I could be a bride for as many hours as possible. I was standing in the back of the church watching my maid of honor and bride maids as they walked down the aisle on the white runner the ushers had just unrolled. My sweetheart Donna was ready in her pretty white gown and with her basket of flowers. She would later in the day ask me if she was married too. I think I broke her heart when I told her no. As I looked down at her, I could tell she was frightened, but she put a smile on her face, just like I asked, and slowly walked to the front of the church.

St. Michaels was a small, old church, but it came to life with the flowers we provided. The beautiful blooms made my wedding day appear as if it was happening in the early chill of spring, instead of winter being just around the corner. Sunlight filtered through the stained-glass windows. Everyone turned as the music picked up for the bridal march. I didn't have anyone else to ask but Tom to walk me down the aisle. Uncle Harry had stayed home in New Jersey with Skip and Ed so Aunt Lina and Aunt Theresa could make the trip. Neither one of the aunts could drive, so it was a very long bus ride for them. I was truly grateful they came. It was a high point of my wedding, to have them with me.

Now it was my turn to walk down the aisle. This was the moment I had dreamed about since I was a little girl. Standing behind the sheer curtain, pretending it was my veil, holding my hands, and clutching Mom's artificial flowers. Now, I had the real thing.

I was in my billowy white gown, with a real veil covering my face. My brown eyes were shining with happiness as I looked to the front of the church and saw the man I ecstatically wanted to spend the rest of my life with. But as perfect as the church service was, the reception had lots of problems.

"Where is the head bridal table," Rusty's mother wanted to know upon entering the hall. "There is no head table for the bride and groom,"

"I thought the caterers took care of that," my mom replied.

I was so worried about the last-minute alterations on my gown that I hadn't even thought about it. I was sure Mom never attended a big wedding, so she wouldn't have known either. But looking over at Rusty's mother's face, I knew it was a big deal to some people. I wouldn't let this setback stress anyone out.

"Just push a couple of tables together, and it'll be fine," I said.

The unknown band we hired was so loud, you had to cup your hands around your mouth to be heard in conversation. Everyone sighed with relief when they took a break. But I didn't care about the problems. I was loving every minute of this until they said it was time for Rusty and me to leave.

"What?" I said, confused. I didn't want to go yet.

In the sixties, it was customary for the bride and groom to eat, have their first dance, cut the cake, and be one of the first ones to leave the reception. Although our leaving was made much easier by the tradition that Rusty's family implemented called "The Money Dance".

If you wanted to dance with the bride, you had to pin money to the bride's dress to help pay for the honeymoon. In our case we didn't have pins, so they opted to have everyone form a line and give the money to Rusty's Aunt Teddy. A couple of people eagerly got in line with wallets and coin purses in hand.

Wow, I like this tradition, I smiled to myself.

I took a turn around the dance floor with my brother Dave and laughed. Aunt Teddy was hilarious. She didn't let anyone dance with me for more than thirty seconds.

"Come on, move it along, time is money," she joked. She had everyone up on their feet and laughing. I couldn't believe the bundle of cash she presented to us after. After the money dance, I was ready to head out.

As Rusty was helping me into the car, we happened to see a body in the back seat. It wasn't until Rusty rolled him over that he realized it was Aunt Teddy's son, Alan. Of all the cars in the parking lot, he had to pick ours to sleep it off. We fussed at him until he woke up startled, dazed, confused, and maybe a little drunk. It was a good laugh at the end of the night.

Chapter 13

We planned to live in Rusty's grandparents' house while they were in Florida for the winter. That would give us a little time to save up money for all the things we would need. In the meantime, I talked to Mom as often as I could on the phone to make sure things were okay at home with my family. This was the first time I was living apart from them, outside of the time I spent in New Jersey with Aunt Lina and Uncle Harry for the adoption.

My younger siblings were still too young to move out on their own, but it seemed that Mom and Tom carried on as usual. Thank goodness it didn't sound like there were any major incidents without me there. But I was always on my guard, and I was focused on my newlywed life with Rusty. We were building something new out of old, fond memories he had.

Rusty loved his grandparents' house. It had been his home away from home. He had grown up across the street.

"Grandma come and get me!" Rusty told me he would yell from his side, and she would come out and guide him across the street.

"Are you hungry, Rusty?" Grandma would say to him.

"Mom didn't feed me," he always told her.

From the pictures of when he was little, it was obvious he was getting a whole lot of extra meals. There was no doubt that Rusty was her favorite, and she let everyone know it. His grandmother was an unstoppable force. She raised a pair of identical twin boys. She named one Donald, who was Rusty's father, and the other twin Don, which was Rusty's uncle. To the world, Don would just be an abbreviation for Donald. She had no idea the problems that would cause.

Donald K Bilger, Don K. K. Bilger, and now my husband is Donald Kay Bilger, but not a junior. They surmised that his dad's middle name was only an initial, so when they named him Donald Kay, well, that was a completely different name. He was Donald Kay until grandma arrived at the hospital.

They told me she had survived three husbands and did whatever she wanted. She said what was on her mind regardless of the fallout from her abrasive comments. I made a point of treating her with a great deal of respect. Not that it was returned. But we both loved Rusty. She was the one that gave him that name.

Rusty's very sweet mother had wanted him to be named Donald after his father. But the minute grandma walked into the hospital room, she declared that he looked like a Rusty with all that red hair that matched her own. So legally it was Donald, but from day one, everyone referred to him as Rusty. When I met him, the red hair was completely gone. It was now as dark as his mother's. I had to ask why they named him Rusty. He laughed when he told me the story.

Rusty's short, red-headed father was always joking around. He was a long-haul truck driver. He would leave at the beginning of the week and return at the end of the week. If he was home for two days, that was a lot. So I thought it would work out well when we decided to live across the street from them.

"Mary honey, we would love it if you would call us mom and dad, but only if you want to," Rusty's mom said to me one afternoon, not long after my wedding.

We just moved into his grandmother's house in Toledo while Rusty's grandparents were still in Florida. The word "Dad" had not crossed my lips for several years now. I didn't think of it as a problem.

My little girl had shut the door on that situation, and I never, ever thought about it. I was elated to call his parents "Mom and Dad," and feel like part of their family. They represented everything good and normal to me. "Normal" was very important to me. I just wanted the mundane daily rituals that I had been craving, instead of the freakish life I had been living before. Alice in Wonderland had nothing on me.

Our first Christmas in 1967 was joyful for me. On the nights Rusty was at apprenticeship school, I would walk across the street and help his mom wrap Christmas gifts. Everything had to be boxed, full of tissue paper, wrapped with beautiful ribbons and handmade decorations. The Christmas balls on his mom's elegant white tree were all hand painted by her. It matched the decor of her living room. During the nights leading up to Christmas, we easily wrapped a hundred gifts. Rusty's Mom bought gifts for everyone. I felt like the luckiest girl in the world.

"So Rusty, what do you want Santa to bring you for Christmas this year," I teased. We were putting ornaments on our own Christmas tree. Everyone had given us some to get us started.

"Well, I need a pair of four-buckle rubber boots. Those construction sites are so damn muddy and cold," Rusty said.

OK, I can handle that, I thought. We had a very small allowance to use for Christmas. I had already bought several things I thought he would like. The boots would fit nicely into my budget. I wanted to get him whatever would make him happy, so this would be easy.

We attended midnight mass at St. Michael's on Christmas Eve with mom and dad. The spirit that filled that church was beyond anything I had ever experienced. I could feel tears welling in my eyes. I had so much to be thankful for this Christmas. As I kneeled and bowed my head, I thanked God for this wonderful new life I was living. I was thankful to finally be out of my mom and Tom's house. I was grateful that my siblings were okay.

I said a prayer of gratitude for Aunt Lina and Uncle Harry for taking me in during my moment of crisis. I also said a prayer of gratitude for baby Christine being adopted. I was also thankful to Rusty's parents for showing me real love and adding good memories to my mind. The life I was living now was the first time that I truly felt loved, without chaos being involved. But no matter how much happiness I was feeling, I couldn't shake the idea that something was going to pop up and take it all away from me.

"Rusty, wake up, it's Christmas!" I smiled.

"Honey, it's still dark outside," he mumbled.

Rusty turned over and pulled the covers tighter around him. What was he thinking? When you wake up, that is the start of Christmas.

"I'll put the coffee and tea on while you wake up," I said.

I tip-toed to the kitchen. Rusty snored peacefully in our bedroom. I smiled to myself. When I was growing up, the Christmas tree lights stayed on all night on Christmas Eve. I kept that tradition going in this home. I wrapped my new bathrobe snugly around me and surveyed our first Christmas tree on Christmas morning.

The Christmas tree was real. I loved the smell of fresh pine coming from the evergreen needles. The white lights were glowing from the night before. The shiny, handmade ornaments were painted in a range of colors. Through the window was a gentle snowfall. But the Christmas tree stood out in my mind the most. Yum, I could eat it up, it looked so perfect to me. Rusty would see it for the first time with the presents under the tree. Last night he asked me to do him a favor.

"Would it be all right if you put all the Christmas presents under the tree so I can see them for the first time on Christmas morning? That's the only way I have ever experienced Christmas," he asked sheepishly.

My big, burly husband was just as much a kid as I was when it came to Christmas. I loved it. I couldn't help it, but I laughed when he asked me that.

"You have never seen presents under your tree before Christmas morning?" I said.

Rusty laughed with me. He shook his head. "I never saw the bags from where Mom bought the stuff. I never saw wrapping paper laying around. There is no difference from when I woke up on Christmas morning when I was five. Mom would wrap whatever she bought and put it away. No matter what time we arrived back home on Christmas Eve, the old man and Mom would lug the presents downstairs while Bill and I went to bed. That never changed."

I thought that was the cutest thing I ever heard. I grinned at him. "You go to bed and I'll be in shortly," I said. "I think it's a great idea."

It took me about two hours before I was completely happy with the room. The presents under the tree were full of shiny ribbons and decorative paper. Now it was time to make sure my husband was awake to enjoy it with me.

"Come on Rusty, you made me wait long enough!" I said.

I tackled him to make sure he was wide awake. He chuckled and flipped open the covers. We made our way to the living room. He marveled at the Christmas tree.

"By the way, we have another custom that's always done on Christmas. Everyone takes turns. You open one present, then I open one," Rusty said.

I saw the mountain of gifts under wraps at his parents' house. I could only imagine how long their Christmas mornings had to last.

"Really? Just one gift at a time and taking turns?" I said.

Rusty shrugged. "Sometimes, we had to stop for lunch and then continue all the way until dinner. Mom shops all year for Christmas. When school would start, we wouldn't get a lot of new clothes because she saved them for Christmas. Christmas has always been wonderful at our house," he said.

Rusty started to open his first present with me on our couch. I was used to all of us kids tearing into the presents at the same time, but this way was a smart way to do it. For me, it allowed me to watch everyone's reactions to their gifts. Our first Christmas tradition was established that morning.

"Just one more to open, Rusty," I said.

I had saved his boots last because I knew he would be happy to get them. They were in a large box because he wore a size twelve. I wrapped them in beautiful paper and added a coordinating big bow, just like his mom had taught me. I did wish she had told me how to correctly decorate my tree. Not only did I put the tree up very early, but I put the biggest, prettiest, ones on the ends of the branches. If the tree were hanging from the ceiling, upside down, it would have a perfect shape.

I took my last sip of tea as Rusty carefully unwrapped the box. He set the bow aside so it could be used again, just like his mother had taught him to do. I was learning a lot about Christmas this morning.

"Galoshes," Rusty said. His voice left no doubt that was not the present he was expecting.

"I thought that was what you wanted for Christmas!" I half cried.

"Well yeah, but not as the last present. The last present is always something very special," Rusty answered.

"But that's what I thought I did, Rusty," I fretted.

"Honey, it's all right, I just had my heart set on a new leather jacket, is all."

"But you never said anything about a jacket, Rusty. And if you had that would have been more than my whole budget for Christmas."

"I know, I know, sweetheart, everything is just fine," Rusty smirked, hands up.

I giggled, hand over my lips. We laughed about it later. What a humorous time we had around the dinner table that night, reliving this new escapade into married life. I had a feeling this story was going to be around for a long, long time. The decorations were barely put away when Rusty's mom went into grandchild mode.

Chapter 14

"Mary, we have a special tradition in our family," Rusty's mom said over coffee one morning when she came to visit.

This family has a lot of traditions, I thought.

"My sisters and I get together and set up the nursery for each of our children's firstborn because it is such a huge expense for you just starting out. Then, if you have more children, you can just pass everything down. We will buy the bed, dressing table, and everything a nursery requires if that's ok with you?" his mom said.

It was more than ok with me. I got out of my seat and gave her a big hug. She chuckled and patted my back. This moment, and the sweet aroma of tea, was another one to add to my pile of good memories that was slowly growing in my mind. This family and their wonderful traditions. This was exactly the family life I had been dreaming about.

"Mary, you will have everything you need when the time comes. We also plan on throwing you a baby shower," she smiled.

70

"Mom, I've never heard of anything so generous, thank you," I gushed.

Mom and her two sisters Aunt Teddy and Aunt Lucy were three very creative, talented ladies. They painted, sewed, and could do any kind of craft project out there. For my wedding, she had made me a satin jacket lined with beautiful, warm white fur.

Mom's oldest sister Lucy taught ceramics for the Adult Board of Education. She ran classes out of her home. Aunt Teddy was the fun one. She was just as creative but more outgoing than the rest of the family. She was the one that got everyone dancing at my wedding reception for the money dance. Aunt Teddy always made me feel happy when I was around her. My baby was certainly going to be well cared for.

I was due in June, and there were a lot of preparations going on. I barely had a bump when I started wearing maternity clothes. Later, I gained fifty pounds and looked more like a beachball than a bump. I was caught up in the preparation of getting everything ready for the baby. But I was not preparing myself for the motherhood part.

I loved the idea of having Rusty's baby, but ice-cold fear was dripping into my mind. It started to overshadow everything. My brain couldn't or wouldn't let me dwell on motherhood. This responsibility was going to be way different than looking out for my little brothers and sister in Mom and Tom's house.

My old, long-lost demon was trying to visit me. My father's mental illness. Because he had it, I believed that I had it too. I thought maybe I had lost this demon when I met Rusty, but apparently not. My father's mental illness lingered on in me like a chameleon. It was there, but not noticeable most of the time. It could jump on my face at any given moment. I knew that if dad could do what he did, he had to be mentally ill. And I felt it coming after me. It wanted to consume me and take my protective little girl away. This monster wanted to make me pay. But for what, I wasn't sure.

Rusty's grandparents came back earlier than anticipated. It was March and they were due back in May.

"We're sorry to barge in unexpected, but we had enough of Florida. Don't worry, you don't have to move out now. We'll stay in the guest room while you're here," Grandma said to us.

The house had a good size living room and dining room, with a nice, large kitchen. The bedrooms were not far apart from each other, and they were rather small. Grandma did comment on how nice the house looked upon returning, except I put away a lot of her tchotchkes. I preferred a cleaner look in a home.

The next few days felt a little uncomfortable for me, having to share living quarters with Rusty's grandma. This was her house after all, and she was a very domineering woman. Her red hair definitively matched her temper. Grandma didn't yell. She used her stare that could bore right through you, along with some very choice, hurtful words. She wasn't a beautiful woman, and her body had that squared-off look. But she did have the legs of a twenty-year-old, and boy could she kill a pair of shorts.

Grandma once told me the story of her father putting her in their wagon and driving her down a dirt road. She said she was about fifteen at the time. He stopped the wagon, then just dropped her off and she was left to fend for herself. No wonder this woman was fierce in all her dealings. I gained immeasurable respect and understanding for her that day. But that didn't mean she was easy to live with.

Rusty and I followed up on all the leads to any place we could afford, but we weren't having much luck. Rusty's mother came to our rescue. She said she knew how hard it was to be around Grandma, and she wanted us to stay at their house until we found something. That took a lot of pressure off us.

On the last night of our living with Grandma, we all decided to go to bed early. Rusty and I were lying in bed talking, when suddenly, Rusty ripped out a loud, awful, smelly fart. I couldn't stand it. I started laughing so hard I thought I would wet my pants, but I couldn't stop.

"Mary, stop it, my grandparents can hear you. God knows what they will think we're doing in here," He worried.

I couldn't answer, I was laughing so hard. Sure enough, a minute later we heard a pounding on our bedroom door.

"What on earth is going on in there? We're trying to sleep!" Grandma fussed.

I covered my mouth with my hands, but my giggling was so infectious that Rusty chuckled along with me, still embarrassed. Thank goodness we were moving across the street the next day. I'm sure grandma and grandpa thought so too.

On the day of the baby shower, which was taking place at Rusty's parents' house, I wasn't feeling well. We had just moved out of mom and dad's place and into our apartment. We were still waiting on some of our new furniture to be delivered.

We had the upstairs apartment of the duplex, and it was only a couple of miles away from both of our families, which made it convenient. It was very clean. For the first time, I was decorating our place. There was a little bedroom right off the living room which would be perfect for the nursery. It stood empty because Rusty's mom assured me it would be complete after the baby shower later today.

I was due at Rusty's cousin Pam's house, to get my hair done for my baby shower. In 1968, the hairdo of the moment was an up-sweep of "petals," or more precisely, big curls on top of the head. This took a considerable amount of time to accomplish. After a few hours of being there, I was becoming very uncomfortable sitting. I got up to walk around and relax. There were no pains in my belly or my back, but my chest felt heavy, as if I was locked in a vice. It felt like my back and front were fighting to get to the middle of my body at the same time.

"Mary, are you sure you're ok?" Pam asked.

I still had a few weeks before my due date, I knew that much. "I'm not in labor, but I feel lightheaded," I told her.

"I think we need to call Rusty and get you checked out," Pam said, more than once.

I tried to assure her that I was not in labor, that it felt like something else. But I couldn't explain what was going on. It seemed like it was only minutes that Rusty was putting me into the car to take me to the hospital. They took me right in, and to everyone's amazement except mine, I was not in labor. The concern was my blood pressure. It was now over 200.

As soon as they got my blood pressure down, I felt so much better. They were admitting me just to be on the safe side. But Rusty's mother and her sisters had worked so hard towards this baby shower. I felt like

I was ruining it. I had no pain. Not in my chest, or in my belly. My mother was with me. She was going to be at the baby shower, but she stayed with me in the hospital. She made it clear that she would call if anything happened, so I kept begging and begging Rusty to go to his mother's and take my place at the baby shower.

Finally, he conceded. Rusty left me in the capable hands of the doctors and nurses. The next day I heard from everyone what a great party it was. I guess Rusty opened the presents and squealed with delight, just like I would have done, just to keep the ladies amused. I could just see my big construction guy, handling the little knit booties and sweaters. I could imagine the befuddled look on his face if he were to open a gift with a breast pump. If that was a present, it would have to be returned. I didn't want any part of pumping milk, not even if it gave me big boobs. What a winner I had for a husband. He wasn't the slightest bit embarrassed and helped make the party a huge success for his mother and aunts. I felt so proud of him.

I expected to go home the next morning. But that night, just before visiting hours were over, I started having pains. I was glad Rusty and my mother were still with me.

"Mary, are you going to make me a daddy tonight?" Rusty asked softly.

"Well, if these pains are any indication, I'm betting on yes," I breathed out.

I could see the smile on his face, and my mother had a very contented smile on as well. She assured me earlier that she was doing okay at home with Tom and the kids. She mostly stayed at home, but sometimes she would go to the bar with Tom. I believed her. I was glad she was here with me. Unlike the last time I gave birth, this time I knew I wasn't alone. Everyone was happy, but I could feel fear drip, drip, dripping, one little thought at a time into my brain. I wasn't sure what I was afraid of.

Chapter 15

Instead of sharing this information, I kept thinking, *I can do this, I can do this.*

When the pains started getting bad, the nurse told us about a machine they had. It was supposed to make the labor pains less intense. It was a device that was strapped over your belly with a clear round dome at the top. When a contraction started, I could push a button that would create a vacuum. That would pull my belly up and give the baby more room to turn, resulting in less pain for me. They gave me the magic button and I lay there with my finger on the trigger, waiting to go into battle with the next contraction. It didn't take long for a big one to hit.

I could see and feel this otherworldly contraption getting tight around my stomach. It pulled my belly higher and higher. It was like watching someone blow up a balloon, to the point where you start to cringe, waiting for the burst to come.

When I got pregnant, I weighed 105 pounds. Nine months later I entered the hospital weighing 155 pounds. I knew how huge I looked.

Now with this alien device on me making my stomach bigger and bigger, we could only stare. Our eyes grew wider as we watched my belly blow up.

Good lord, where are they going to pop this baby out of me? I worried.

The contraction ended, and my stomach started coming back down. Then my crazy husband started laughing and laughing until tears were dripping from his eyes.

"Mary, there must be a twenty-pound baby in there!"

He couldn't stop laughing. I didn't find it funny at all.

"Just get out Rusty!" I growled at him.

"Oh honey, I'm sorry," Rusty said. "It's just--Mary, That is the biggest belly I have ever seen."

Oh boy, that was not the right thing to say to me at that moment. I had been very sensitive about all the weight I gained, and now with him standing there telling me that, my husband left me fuming mad. I couldn't stand looking at his red face full of laughter.

"Go out to the waiting room, I don't want you in here with me. Just sit with the family," I told him.

"But I said I was sorry," Rusty blinked, confused.

"*Out,*" I said.

Rusty quietly left the room. I went back into battle with my labor pains. I breathed in and out steadily. I used that stupid machine for a couple more contractions. I was still in pain. I wanted it out of my room. It was useless. I'd been in labor almost seven hours before they wheeled me to the delivery room. In 1968 you went into the delivery room all by yourself. No husband, no mother, and no friend. I had given my best, but I wasn't sure if I could get it done. Thankfully, a short time later the doctor came in, ready to deliver our twenty-pound baby.

"Mary, you're doing a great job and it's almost over. We're going to give you a saddle block anesthesia. Before you know it, the baby will be in your arms."

That saddle block gave me instantaneous relief, but I had to make sure I remained flat on my back for the next twenty-four hours, because if I didn't, there was a great possibility that I could suffer long-term problems with headaches. I would have given my husband and everything I owned to get some relief from the contractions. A few minutes passed. The doctor coached me to push. We were almost to the finish.

"Mommy, you have yourself a son! He has all his fingers and toes," the doctor cheered.

I smiled, sweating and exhausted. I watched as the nurse took the baby over to get his measurements. He was six pounds and thirteen ounces, and twenty-one inches long. He had hair, and it wasn't red. A nurse smiled at me.

"Everything looks good," she said.

I watched her. She had just said that. Something started happening to me. My whole body was convulsing. The nurse's face was suddenly inches away from mine, close enough that I could see the panic in her eyes. She vanished from my line of sight.

"Doctor!" the nurse yelled.

Then everything went black.

I finally regained consciousness. My eyes were dry and scratchy. My body felt sore. There was a nurse posted in a chair next to my bed. I wasn't in ICU, although we had insurance. We couldn't use the maternity portion of the insurance because we were not on the plan for a full nine months. We were paying, but we couldn't use it. Everything that happened tonight, was paid out of pocket. As soon as my eyes fluttered open, the nurse went to get Rusty. He walked in with a look of uneasiness on his tired, strained, face.

"You did it, sweetheart. You made me a father," Rusty said. He bent over to hold me.

"What happened, Rusty? I remember delivering the baby, and then my whole body started shaking," I said quietly.

"Dr. Selles said you went into convulsions right after they told you the baby was fine. He didn't understand why it happened. He's going to be running all kinds of tests to find out exactly what happened. How do you feel now? You really gave us a scare."

"I'm tired," I answered honestly.

I wasn't sure about the rest of my feelings. I felt fear still drip and drip in the back of my brain. The rest of the family came in two at a time, because those were the rules. When my mom came in, I felt such relief to see her. All I knew at that time, was a deep desire for my mom to be with me and to take care of me.

"Mary, when I heard that code go out over the intercom last night for doctors to come to maternity, I knew without a doubt that code was for you. I had a terrible feeling I was losing you," Mom said.

I didn't know what to say to that. What had happened to me? I hoped Dr. Selles could tell me. My family was scared for me. I was scared too.

The moment finally arrived; We were going to meet our son. We had named him Robert. We just liked that name. We knew he would not have any form of the name Donald and no middle name of Kay or K or KK. His middle name would be Allen. Everyone always wondered if Grandma had a subliminal message in that KKK middle name thing.

The nurse carried Robert to us. He had his little head of dark hair sticking out of his blanket. He was asleep, so we got to marvel at his pretty face and perfect complexion. Our son was six pounds and thirteen ounces of perfection.

As I was feeding him, I started to feel panicky again. I couldn't relate to what was happening at this moment. I was supposed to share and grow a maternal bond with my son. But fear told me something different. *This innocent child is going to be in my care. I'm responsible for this new life. I'm responsible.*

I remembered every time I had to be responsible for a younger life when I was just a little girl. I was watching my younger brothers. They accidentally hurt themselves while playing. But I was responsible, so it was my fault. I was responsible before I was ready. I am responsible for this tiny, fragile life. There was no way out. I wasn't ready. I couldn't do this. I was a horrible person, and I was going to fail again.

The thoughts wouldn't leave me alone. My heart felt like ice shards were stuck inside my chest. I could feel it pounding, more urgent. I was inwardly freaking out while trying to maintain an outward appearance of calm for everyone. *Someone, please take this beautiful, sweet child away from me. He deserves better than me. He would be better off with anyone but me.*

I'm not equipped to do this.

All these thoughts were running through my mind so fast that I was at a loss for what to do. What was wrong with me? Why was I feeling like this? I couldn't "will" this fear away. Without even thinking about it, my inner system automatically kicked in to save us both. I pressed the button to call the nurse. She came in a moment later.

"Is everything okay?" the sweet nurse asked me.

"Can you please take the baby? I'm not feeling well. I think I might be a little tired," I said in a tranquil voice.

That wasn't the truth, but my insides shaking in fear was. The nurse gently took baby Robert out of my arms. I couldn't do anything, but my little girl could. And she did. After I went home, my inside feelings and my outside actions rarely matched up. I was scared all the time. I had a baby to care for, meals to plan, a house to clean, laundry to do, and I was always so tired.

Chapter 16

My mom had my siblings to take care of at home a mile from our apartment. It would never have crossed her mind to come give me a hand. Rusty's mother had to take care of Bill, who was still in high school. Rusty worked, so it was just me taking care of the baby and the house. It didn't take long for my friend Linda to come to my rescue, along with her husband Jerry.

Linda's staying with me for the first few weeks after I came home from the hospital saved my life. Linda was my friend from high school. She had bright red hair and blue eyes. Best of all, she was always laughing. She could find humor in anything. Her husband Jerry was Rusty's best friend. We played cards on most weekends and spent a lot of time together. But this was one of the kindest things she could have done for me.

No one knew how hard I was trying to hold on to my sanity. I know I couldn't have made it without her. I was short-tempered and hurting, but she never once told me how awful I was being. I was very lucky to have someone so kind and so generous with their time. But that was the kind of person Linda was. I didn't have anyone else to lean on at the time. Everyone was busy with their own lives.

"Mary, when I get pregnant, I'm going to assemble the crib right inside the front door so Jerry can see it as soon as he walks through the door," Linda told me one day as we watched TV in the living room. I laughed with her.

One of the guys Rusty worked with not only gave us this beautiful TV, but carried it upstairs to our apartment and plugged it in. Rusty had a lot of friends like that. I was grateful that we each had a kind friend to help us out at the time. The first night Linda and Jerry stayed over, I heard the baby cry. Linda stopped me on my way to get Robert.

"Mary, this is the reason I'm here. Go back to bed and get some rest. I've got this under control," Linda said. I sighed gratefully and went back to bed.

Sometimes I would watch how Linda took care of the baby. I could tell how much she loved holding and feeding Robert. I could see it on her face. She stayed with me for a few weeks until I felt stronger.

Rusty was a "hands-off dad" throughout this time. Most men were in the late 60s. One time I was at a baby shower. We were in the middle of a game where you tried to get the exact amount of toilet paper that you thought would go around the mother-to-be. The closest to one wrap around her belly would win. The ladies chatted over the music playing in the living room. I giggled as my friend's attempt to wrap the mother-to-be's belly snapped halfway. She threw her hands up in the air but laughed with us.

The doorbell rang. "I'll get it!" I said.

I answered the door. Rusty stood there holding Bob.

"Mary, the baby needs to have his diaper changed," he said. He looked desperate. I took in his and Bob's appearance, bemused. Rusty had grabbed his jacket in a hurry.

"Is it that bad? Goodness, it smells like it," I joked.

The ladies behind me laughed and waved him in. I took the baby from his arms. Rusty sighed.

"I had to crack open a window," he admitted. I chuckled at him.

Rusty wasn't any different from any other husband. He provided for his family. He loved his son and wife. Those were his responsibilities. My responsibility was to maintain the home, care for our baby, and make sure food was hot, ready, and on time. In the back of my mind, it felt like I was juggling while walking a tightrope. I didn't have the first clue how to be successful at this without falling. I didn't know if there was a net to catch me.

I tried to do everything right as a housewife and mother. I focused on Robert, but then the house didn't get cleaned. I couldn't keep up with the laundry. My dinners weren't very good. One day, Rusty's grandmother came over to watch Robert, so I could go to a doctor's appointment. She nailed me as soon as I returned.

"Don't you ever clean your stove?" she wanted to know.

She must have forgotten how clean I kept her place when I lived there. I was embarrassed and hurt. But that was grandma. The bad part for me was that she wasn't lying.

Being scared stiff is a real thing. I woke up in the middle of the night a few weeks after Linda left. Rusty snored peacefully beside me. Robert was asleep in his crib. I lay on my side, fully awake, when a continuous critique started playing in my head. Fear set in. *Drip, drip, drip.* One little thought at a time.

"I am not a good mother. I am not a good wife. I'm not in control of anything. I can't do this anymore."

I couldn't shut off the stream of negative thoughts. It was making me more and more panicky. I couldn't push these thoughts or my feelings to the back of my mind. I tried to make myself think of other things, but that didn't help. I just laid there and endured the onslaught. Fear dripped into my mind before. This time, it felt like the room filled up with ice water. I was struggling to keep my mouth and nose clear so I could breathe.

I couldn't roll over. I couldn't stand up. And this went on and on until I realized I was frozen stiff with fear. If the house had been on fire, I could not have gotten out of bed to run for safety. Light started filtering into the bedroom. My eyes finally closed.

I didn't want Rusty to know how messed up I was. I had no words to explain what happened to me. How can you explain something like this? I thought I was starting to lose it. But I convinced myself that I just had to try harder.

I never said a word to anyone about what happened that night. But I came away with a new truth after that experience. I was a fake.

I watched myself "try" and be a good wife, which I knew wasn't true. I watched myself "try" to be a good, loving mother. But I knew I wasn't. I tried to convince myself everything was going to be fine. I hoped that would be true. Because I would rather be dead than be crazy like my father. I loved my son, but I was not good mother material. I took care of him, and I loved him. Robert gave me his first smile as Rusty was helping me into the car on one hot, July day. As Rusty put him back in my arms, I looked down and saw him smiling. I was worried Rusty was going to miss this. He kept smiling and smiling and my heart was aching with joy. Unfortunately, his daddy didn't get to see it. I held him. I enjoyed all of his little firsts, but I still felt like someone "trying" to be a good mother. I knew I wasn't.

Time did not improve my feelings. I had episodes of feeling like I couldn't breathe. My heart would start racing. It got so bad that I was going to the emergency room a couple of times a week. Rusty put me in the car during an episode I struggled to breathe. I heard some of the family outside whispering and watching.

Rusty looked tired and worried, but he shut my passenger side door and soldiered on. On top of what I was going through, I felt their stares and my shame. I was aware that the family thought I was doing it to get attention. But no matter how many times the hospital told me I was just hyperventilating, the next time it happened, it felt like I was drawing my last breath all over again. I staggered along through life for the next few months, trying to be the person I thought I should be, trying to endure what was happening to me. *I have to try harder*, I thought.

Rusty found us a cute little house with a backyard for Robert about a year later. It was located just around the corner from his parents' house. The bedroom in our old apartment had been very large, so we bought oversized dressers and nightstands to fill the room. It was a very Mediterranean design, with lots of drawers for clothes.

But moving into our "doll house," as I referred to it, created a predicament for this big furniture. Now we could sit on the bed and pull a dresser drawer open to get our clean undies out without taking a step. And if we turned to the other side, we could sit and take care of brushing our hair or putting makeup on. It took some maneuvering to get to the closet. We had a whopping eight to ten inches to get to the closet. If we moved carefully and went sideways, we could manage.

Rusty's mom and her sisters put together the sweetest nursery. Light blue and yellow were Robert's colors. She even made a teddy bear lamp in yellow and white that had his name and the date inscribed on it. The nursery was only about fourteen feet from our bedroom.

With the house being so small, it always looked cluttered. I tried to keep it as nice as I could, but I was losing all interest. I was constantly feeling overwhelmed by everything. And I knew Rusty was frustrated with me. He grimaced at the smell of spaghetti and meatballs coming from the kitchen. He'd just gotten home from work. Robert was in his highchair so I could keep an eye on him. I brought out the plates and saw Rusty's expression.

"What's wrong?" I asked.

"This is the third night this week, Mary. I was just kind of hoping there'd be steak tonight," Rusty said.

"Oh, I'm sorry," I said.

I forgot he asked me to make steak for dinner. And last week, I stretched out vegetable soup, which was easier to make. Rusty sighed and opened the fridge instead of sitting down. I set out the plates. I'd made enough spaghetti to stretch out this week too. Rusty barely touched it.

One evening I had Robert in bed for the night. The house was quiet. A beautiful sunset spread across the sky outside the window. But inside, a pile of clothes spilled over from the laundry basket. The stove needed cleaning. And dishes filled the sink since lunch. Only two cups were clean on the rack. Rusty was out with friends after work. I surveyed every little thing from the living room of my cute "doll house". I just started crying and crying. *I can't do this anymore!*

I had everything I ever dreamed about. Why wasn't I happy? I didn't want to live another day. I was trying to fight this thought dripping into my head. I was losing.

I got the phone book out. I thought there might be a helpline for people in this kind of emergency. If there was, I couldn't find it. In 1968, no one talked about mental health. It was too late for me to call anyone I knew. The sky outside was dark now.

I walked into the bathroom, still crying. I pulled out all the medications. I didn't know what they were. I was just going to take all of them. I had taken about six or eight pills when I heard the door shut. I gasped. What do I do now? Rusty's coming in jolted some sense into me. Could I just go to bed and be all right? What would happen when I told him? I rushed out of the bathroom. Tears streamed down my face.

"Rusty, I just did something stupid!" I cried.

I told him what I had done. He hid his surprise under a veneer of calm. He hadn't even taken his jacket off yet.

"We need to get you to the hospital and get checked out. I'll call Mom to come get Bob," Rusty said.

Thank goodness I didn't take enough to warrant them pumping my stomach. The hospital released me to go home that night.

"I think she just did it to get attention, but I also think she should see a psychiatrist," the doctor told Rusty. And that was that!

I saw the suggested psychiatrist a few times. He was located about twenty minutes from our house. It was a rather small, well-kept building with parking out front. The waiting room was stereotypical of any waiting room. The floor was made up of a white grid with patches of a black pattern. Half of the walls were beige on the bottom half. A coatrack stood in one corner. There was only one painting on the wall of a pasture, and a small side table of magazines. I didn't feel like thumbing through the pages for the latest fashion trends. Pretty soon, the nurse called my name.

The doctor's office was about the same. It was plain and clinical. He sat behind a desk. I faced him like a misbehaved student in the principal's office, instead of a person that needed answers, and help.

"Hello Mary, I'm Dr. Honny. What brings you in today?" he asked.

"I got a referral to see you, because…because I…" I hesitated.

As soon as I started talking, I started sobbing. I didn't share very much with him that day.

Dr. Honny sighed 15 minutes into my appointment with him. "Mary, please step into the restroom and wash your face before going out to the waiting room. I wouldn't want anyone thinking I abused you in here."

I looked at him. He might have been kidding, but I felt embarrassed nevertheless. Dr. Henny also took a personal call while in the middle of our discussions in follow-up appointments.

"Yeah, a nice steak and a big green salad," was his answer to whomever he was talking with through the corded telephone on his desk.

I sat there staring at him, silent. I went back a few more times, but I knew he wasn't the answer to my problems.

Chapter 17

I could tell Rusty had enough of me, but he wasn't innocent either. From the beginning, he was a very hard worker and provided very well for us. It would not be an exaggeration to say work was everything to him. But somehow, he could still find the time to stop for beers after work, hang out, and play cards with his buddies.

He never changed a diaper, bathed Bob, or put him to bed. The most he did was occasionally feed him after he went on baby food. Rusty seemed to be spending more and more time out with his buddies. I tried to squeeze in some couple time for the two of us, even a double-date game night. Dinner was in the oven, but the house wasn't ready for company yet. I still needed to get ready. The kitchen phone rang, and I picked it up. It was Rusty. By now, his shift was almost done.

"Damn Rusty, we have Linda and Jerry coming over tonight! I have so much to do. Can you give me a hand when you get in?" I said.

Rusty hesitated. "I'm just going down to the A&D to meet the guys for a few hours. I won't be that long."

I paused. "Rusty, did you forget about the game night? I thought I mentioned it this morning."

"I don't know. Maybe we should reschedule." Tiredness laced his words.

Rescheduling was a good idea since maybe we both were in over our heads. But then what would I do in the house with Bob, alone? He'd be out with the same friends, sharing drinks for the third time this week. I hadn't seen Linda and Jerry in a while. I missed them. I missed us.

"No, I still want us to have a good time with Linda and Jerry. If you can just come home and help me out a little, it should be fine," I pressed.

Rusty asked what needed to be done to make the game night happen. With a flicker of hope, I listed off the things that needed to be put away or put out of the way. Bob needed to be fed, we should have a quick dinner, and set up snacks for our guests. That was outside of getting dressed, touching up my makeup, and him taking a shower before Linda and Jerry came over, but I didn't mention that last part because it was a given.

There was a long pause over the phone. I could hear the background noise through the phone. Footsteps, people chatting, and the distant sound of construction equipment outside the trailer office.

"Rusty? Did you get all that?" I said.

"Golly, Mary. That's a lot. Why haven't you done any of that before 5 o'clock?"

I felt a prickle in the back of my mind. I had so much to do, all the time. "That's why I'm asking for your help, Rusty."

Rusty sighed. "Mary, I can't do this. Just tell them we're sorry and reschedule. I'll be home in a few hours, okay?"

"Why? So you can go drink with your buddies, again?" I snapped.

"The house isn't clean and you've been home all day? That doesn't make any sense. Sometimes I wish I never married you," Rusty muttered.

I sucked in a breath. "Well, sorry I'm not perfect," I bit out.

I could hear his chair squeak. I could imagine him rubbing his eyes, leaning back in his chair.

"Tell Linda and Jerry I'm sorry to miss out. If you really want company, just do what you can. Don't leave a plate out for me."

Rusty hung up shortly after that. I stared at the phone in my hand. His going out was starting to become a regular thing. I always had so much to do and little time for myself. I didn't know what to do.

I did the most horrible thing a wife can do – I went to his mother to help me out that night. He truly thought he was justified in doing what he wanted when I needed help. Rusty's mom was able to take care of Bob while I spent time with Linda and Jerry. I told them Rusty made other plans. But I couldn't enjoy our time together. Not with an empty seat at the kitchen table. Not when he just said that to me. I realized this life I was living, the one I dreamed of, wasn't working.

"Mary, what the hell were you thinking going to my mother?" Rusty argued the day after.

"I was thinking maybe, she could make you understand that this isn't working. I'm as miserable as you are, and I've had enough!"

I knew I had to make some changes. I was in my early twenties. To me, it felt like I never had a life of my own. I wanted and needed a "Mary life". I wanted to make my own money, hang out with my friends, and have a little breathing room in my life.

My first point of business was to talk to one of Bob's three doting grandmas about taking care of him while I worked. They lived straight down the street from each other. My mom was about eight blocks down but within walking distance from my house. She was the grandma on the end of the street we lived on. Rusty's mom was grandma on the side of the street to us. It was always funny to us how close the three of them were to our little doll house with Bob.

We called them grandma on the side, grandma in the middle, and grandma on the end. I went to "grandma in the middle", which was Rusty's grandma. I asked her if she would like to watch Bob for me. I offered this to her as a paid position, but I knew she would have paid me to have him with her every day.

I found the unlikely and fun job of a store detective. I couldn't believe how easy it was for me to catch a thief. For the most part, I could blend in very well with the customers. I didn't wear jeans or tennis shoes or a ball cap. I wore nice, conservative dresses or slacks.

Sometimes I even wore small, heeled shoes like a lot of our customers did. The best part was the uncanny way I could sense which customers were going to steal.

It was the nervousness I sensed about them. I think because I had so much experience with the feelings of fear and anxiety in my own life, I could understand the signs in another person. I could tune into that feeling like a cat knowing when to pounce.

I watched a lady paw through a selection of shirts under the bright, department store lights. It was barely sunset outside. Most shoppers came in for the weekend sale. I browsed a selection of slacks, casually keeping an eye out for the woman in a blue top. I'd seen the look in her eyes. She was checking the doors and the register too often. Her movements had the same tell of a woman that wanted to bolt. I angled my body toward the doors. The woman stuffed two shirts into her purse when no one else was looking. She power-walked toward the door. I bumped into her. She blinked, startled and nervous.

"Oh! I'm sorry," she began.

Before she could dash around me, I flashed my security badge. "I'm sorry too. Will you come with me, please?" I smiled.

The woman's face lost all her color.

I was a hundred and ten pounds of fearlessness. It was a game that I loved to play. I was made Security Manager within the year. Of course, the store isn't constantly filled with bad guys, so it gave me time to talk to the clerks and managers in each department. I was loving this job. A group of us started going out to lunch. Or, if we were working the evening hours, we would make plans to go out to a club and dance. I had a few laughs and social drinks. I bummed a cigarette to try the taste of the smoke. I was living a "Mary life," and I did not feel guilty.

I loved my husband, and I loved my son, but this new freedom was intoxicating. I wanted more and more of it. Before long, I wanted a divorce. I wasn't after the house or his pensions. I knew Bob would be better off with his father and my in-laws. I would still be very much involved in Bob's life. I didn't want to hurt anyone, but I knew how essential this was for me.

I got a divorce in our seventh year of marriage when my son was the same age. I had my own place. But I gave up being a store detective. There was a bunch of women that were working together to hit the big department stores. If they got caught, they had razor blades. They were using them on the detectives to escape. This was no longer a game.

Chapter 18

My next job was at a new truck dealership. I was the secretary to the Secretary-Treasurer of the company. I took care of Payroll and Accounts Receivable, among other things. I liked being in the new building with everything so pristine. It was a peaceful environment. I even bought a new car from another dealership connection at an unbelievably low price. Life was good. I just had one problem. I couldn't stay away from Rusty and Bob.

That was fine with them. In the beginning, I would go over to the house and put Bob's outfits together for the school week. The teacher knew of our situation. One Sunday afternoon I came over. Bob was a young boy now, so the nursery had lost some of its baby touches. But the colors of the room stayed the same, sunshine yellow and sky blue. Rusty watched me set out clothes from the doorway.

"Did I tell you the teacher asked if I was the one that dressed Bob for school in the mornings? She said he's always the best-dressed student in the class."

"What did you tell her?" I asked curiously.

He grinned sheepishly. "I said yes. Didn't know what else to say."

I let out a small chuckle. "Well, I guess you were technically truthful. But you do remember how colored blind you are, right?"

"How can I forget? It's true," Rusty said.

The both of us laughed. A moment passed between us. I cleared my throat and went back to my task. Rusty left me be. Said he'd fix me a cup of tea.

I was enjoying the freedom of being on my own, coming and going as I pleased. As happy as that made me, it equally hurt being away from Bob. He told his teacher that he lost his mommy. I found out about it from Rusty. That truly broke my heart. I made as much room as I could for Bob in my new life.

The apartment I had rented had a built-in pool. Bob would come over and spend the weekends with me. He loved the pool as much as I did when I was his age. Then the three of us started spending more and more time together. Bob's happiness was Rusty's and mine's prime concern in co-parenting our child. We did everything we thought would make him happy. We bought him anything he wanted because we were determined that he would have a good childhood. Rusty didn't have much of a childhood either.

At a very early age, he wanted to work and make money. He would head to the family's farm in Marion, Ohio, as soon as school was out in June. He'd come back right before school started in September. This is what he wanted to do with his summers and Rusty loved it. Rusty grew up fast for different reasons than I did. But we both wanted Bob to be a child as long as he wanted. My world was split in two, and I was just one person, one girl. Could I be a mother, and still live just for myself?

I tried my hardest to reconcile wanting a life of my own and still wanting my family life. It was wrong and it was selfish. It came to an end when I started seeing a guy in my building. I realized I was going to have to come to terms with what I was doing. I had to make a choice.

I backed off from spending so much time with Rusty. I started a relationship with Richard, a guy that lived down the hall from me. We dated for several months. I met his parents and we all got along fine. Then Richard thought we should introduce Bob to his parents.

"I'm not so sure about this," I admitted.

Bob had been around Richard several times when we were at the pool, but nothing more than that.

"Mary, he is your son, and I would like to get to know him. When you get Bob this weekend, plan on the two of you coming over here on Saturday night for dinner. I'll invite my parents," Richard said.

"I don't know about this," I said.

But I eventually agreed. I thought this might be a good thing. I told Bob about the plans. He made a face. He was not thrilled about spending time with grown-ups he didn't know, but Bob agreed to go with me. I reminded him to use his manners and to be sure to say, "please" and "Thank you".

At six o'clock, we walked down the narrow hallway and knocked on Richard's door. Richard opened it with a big smile on his face. He waved down at Bob, who was standing in front of me.

"Come on in partner," Richard said cheerfully.

Bob took exaggerated, slow, slow steps through the door. I was right behind him. Heat rose to my cheeks. I had a bad feeling about this. I pushed my nerves away. Richard was puzzled but soldiered on.

"Bob, these two people sitting over there are my parents, Connie and Sam. Folks, this is Mary's son, Bob."

"It's nice to meet you, Bob," Connie and Sam said in unison.

My little stinker wouldn't speak. He stood in the apartment, and carefully glanced around the room. He wrinkled his nose. Richard quickly ushered all of us to the dinner table. Connie pulled out a roast chicken roast from the oven and Richard sent out her vegetable medley. Bob sat next to me. Richard was on my other side. Connie and Sam sat on the other side of Bob, completing our little circle at the table.

"So, how do you like school?" Richard asked.

My eyes darted to Bob. I silently willed him to open his mouth.

"It's ok," Bob said. He looked at no one in particular. Bob poked the green beans with his fork.

"Do you like sports?" Sam asked.

"I play on a hockey team," Bob intoned.

"Are you any good?" Connie pressed, with a little smile.

"Well, that's a stupid question," Bob replied.

I gasped. "Bob, mind your manners and apologize," I told him. My face went crimson with embarrassment. Bob's brows pinched together, the picture of polite confusion.

"But it is a stupid question, Mom. I couldn't have made the team if I wasn't good."

Oh God, please open the floor so I can fall through it, I begged.

My eyes looked at Richard, begging him to start a new topic with anyone else. My precocious son was on a roll, and he knew exactly what he was doing. I swear there was a twinkle in his eye. At least while we were eating, he used his good table manners. Richard politely changed the subject to ask me how my work week was going. I smiled and jumped right in, praising Connie for her delicious dish. Bob stayed quiet. But when dessert arrived, he started in again.

"What is that? It looks disgusting," Bob said. He eyed the red velvet cake Richard brought out.

"Bob, it's red velvet cake. You've had it before and you liked it," I answered.

"It looks like it was made with blood. I think they put blood in it, Mom."

He made a face. I huffed at him. "Bob, that's enough. Eat your cake and be quiet."

I could see the look passing back between Richard's parents. It was somewhere between amusement and disbelief. This was not going well. My face was still heated. They brought cards out after dinner. Bob said to Sam, "I can play cards."

"You can? Can you do any card tricks?" Sam asked.

"Yep, just watch," Bob said.

Sam and Bob sat at the dining table. Bob shuffled the deck and handed it to Sam to cut. the rest of us watched Bob as he shuffled the deck again. He fanned out the cards in front of Sam face down.

"Pick a card, remember what it looks like, then put it back," Bob said.

Sam peeked at a card in the middle, his hand covering the back. The rest of us glanced at it too. Sam returned the card to the deck. Bob slapped all the cards together and shuffled the deck with nimble fingers. He flicked out a card. It was a queen of spades, the exact one Sam picked out.

"Is this it?" Bob asked.

Sam's brows rose. Connie clapped her hands in delight. All of us were impressed.

Sam smiled. "That was really good Bob! It was so good I'm going to give you a dollar for showing it to me."

Sam reached into his pocket and pulled out his wallet.

"Keep it. I don't need your money. My daddy has plenty," Bob quipped.

I let out a horrified squeak and stood up. "I am so sorry; he doesn't usually act like this!"

I grabbed Bob's hand and headed toward the door. I didn't get out soon enough, because before leaving Bob looked at Richard and said, "Your mom is really fat."

"Bob!" I cried, my voice near Minnie Mouse levels. I was red from my scalp down to my neck. I knew I'd replay that dinner a few times before I went to sleep.

I loved Rusty and I loved Bob, but I also loved this new freedom I was experiencing for the first time in my life. But it was selfish, and it had to stop. We had been divorced for a year.

Chapter 19

I dropped Bob off at Rusty's house later that night. As flustered as I was, I told him what happened in Richard's living room. Rusty had sent Bob to get ready for bed.

"Mary, this is crazy. We can't stay out of each other's lives. I love you so much, and I know without a doubt you love me too. Just come back home. We can make this work."

I couldn't answer him then. A part of me wanted to talk to my mother about it, but I couldn't bring myself to talk about it over the phone with her. Her choices between her relationship with Tom versus her family life still had painful echoes in my heart. I did not feel like facing them. This was about me, Rusty, and Bob. I talked on the phone with Linda the next day. She was quiet for a moment.

"Mary, all you have to do is ask yourself one question. What makes you the happiest, and don't stop to think about any of the details. When are you the most content?"

"When I'm with Rusty and Bob," I said without hesitation.

"There's your answer. All you need to do is fine-tune the problems you were having in the marriage."

That gave me a lot to think about. I figured the problems in the marriage were caused by my mental baggage. This past year made me realize how much I loved and wanted to be with my family. If there had to be a choice, and there certainly did, I wanted my family. I had a year of my "Mary Life". My family won hands down. I also knew this choice was going to hurt Richard. I didn't realize how serious this relationship was to him. He never liked how much time I spent with Bob and Rusty, but I really didn't give him any choice in the matter. It had been a bad idea, allowing Bob to meet Richard's parents.

The more time went on, the more I could see how my relationship with Richard and my "Mary life" was affecting Bob. It didn't sit well with me in my heart, how my choices were affecting my beautiful son. I did not want to make the same choices as my mother did when she put herself before her children, due to her hurts. I needed to face Richard sooner or later. I needed to put an end to what I was doing.

The next time I stopped by the house, Bob was at the farm with his grandparents. He loved the farm as much as his dad did. Bob's pet cow was called "Gus". As soon as he closed the door to the car, Bob would run and say, "Hi!" to Gus the cow.

I was far from being a country girl, but that farm was inviting. Rusty had told me before about working on the farm.

"Mary, I couldn't wait to get out of school in June to work on the farm. It was really hard work but I loved it. I always wanted to have a farm with horses."

"Boy, I'm glad you changed your mind honey," I told him at the time.

I shivered thinking of being in a stall with those huge monsters called horses.

When I was little, I was taken to the hospital once to get some stitches in my foot. Another little girl was waiting to be seen that had been bitten by a horse, on her face. She was screaming so bad that I couldn't stand it. So, I never developed any warm fuzzy feelings toward horses in general.

The big farmhouse and several, well cared for buildings. The Isler family were cousins to Rusty. They farmed several thousand acres in

Marion, Ohio. There were miles and miles of green corn stalks. They waved in the fresh breeze. There was a bright red barn and a low, flat horse stable. The buildings were kept pristine. The workers drove tractors in organized sections. Gus the cow grazed peacefully in her fenced-off area. The air smelled fresh and cool. Just looking out over the expanse, I felt peace. The Isler family waved to me from the front porch of the house. I smiled at them.

Much later, Rusty and I sat in our--I mean his--kitchen. We had a home built in Shoreland before Bob started going to school. We didn't want him in the Toledo school system at the time. Rusty handed me a cup of tea. For a moment I wished I had something stronger to drink to give me a little courage, but I had time to think about this.

"Rusty, do you think we can make this work?" I asked.

He gave me a long, searching look. I swallowed. Nerves prickled across my skin, but I had to get this out.

"I didn't have any emotional problems this past year. That says a lot, don't you think?"

"Mary, you just needed to be young and carefree for a while. Let's get married and start all over again. What do you say?" Rusty said.

Before I could say yes or no, he jumped up and went to the cupboard. Rusty came back with a twisty tie from a loaf of bread. He twisted it into a ring and put it on my bare ring finger. I didn't have to think about it for another second.

"Yes!" I said.

Rusty grinned. I locked my arms around his neck. He gave me a soft kiss. It'd been long enough. I felt right in his arms. I knew I would savor this feeling later. I didn't go back to my apartment that weekend.

It was Sunday night when I went back to my apartment. Ten minutes later there was a knock on my apartment door. Richard was at the door. The hallway was quiet. His eyes were concerned and anxious.

"Mary, did something happen to Bob that kept you over there all weekend?"

I took a deep breath. The time had come to break the news.

"No Richard," I said. "Bob was away for the weekend. Rusty and I did some soul searching. We decided to work things out between us. We believe we can make it work this time, and it would be so much better for Bob."

I looked up and saw tears running down his face. My mouth popped open. I hadn't realized he was that serious about our relationship.

"Mary, I hope you know what you're doing. I don't know why you think it will work this time. Nothing has changed," Richard said, his voice thick.

I almost reached for him. But I knew it wouldn't be right.

"Richard, I'm sorry. I didn't mean to hurt you, but I have to do this. My lease is up on the apartment this month. I'll start moving my things out next week."

His face crumpled. He turned on his heel and walked back to his apartment. I watched until his door closed. The sound echoed in the halls. Did I say it right? Did I hurt him too badly? I don't know. Richard left on vacation that week. I never saw him again.

Chapter 20

For the next few months, we stayed in our self-made cocoon. We didn't socialize very much with family and friends, because not everyone was happy for us. Bob was happy. Rusty was happy. I was happy. To us, that was what mattered. We thought the family needed time to adjust to this change. We knew they loved and cared about us. In time, hopefully they would see we had to be together.

Rusty and I decided we would get married in Miami and book a cruise for our honeymoon. We made special arrangements for Bob to fly into Orlando after our cruise. The three of us would spend five days at Disney World, which had opened just a couple of years earlier. We figured we could get a marriage license and be joined at the courthouse. We just wanted this to be easy and fun.

If you believe in fate, it would seem like everything was working for us. The day we arrived at the hotel, there was a booth set up with colorful pamphlets of palm trees and beaches. A woman came out from behind the booth with a welcoming smile.

"Hi, I'm Samantha. Are the two of you booking today?" she asked.

"Yes, we just got in from Ohio," I smiled back.

Samantha wanted to know how long we'd be staying. Then somehow, the conversation turned to time-share ownership.

"That is the last thing we need right now," we told her. We started explaining all that we had to do and the short time in which to do it.

"I think we can help each other out. I have a very good friend that's a judge. If I can get her to marry you on Saturday at her home, would you two go to the presentation? You don't have to buy anything. I'll get the credit for just sending you there," Samantha promised.

That sounded like an answer to one problem, so we agreed. The next morning, Samantha made the arrangements for us to be at the timeshare. We believed Samantha was being honest with us. After all, we knew where to find her if she wasn't.

The next morning, a van was waiting to take us to see the time-shares at ten o'clock on the dot. We figured we would get this over with fast and head to the beach. Three hours later, the time-share people were still pressuring us. They kept bringing in a new salesman to make a pitch at us. This was some real high-pressure selling. They had driven us there, so we couldn't just walk out. We could have been there for another few hours if the newest salesman had stopped to think before he called me "honey" in the middle of his spiel. Rusty's face turned red.

"Who the hell do you think you're talking to calling my wife, honey? We're leaving now. And that damn van better be out front waiting for us!" Rusty barked.

The salesman backed away, eyes wide and cheeks tinted pink. "I'm so sorry sir. I didn't see a ring on her hand."

I didn't know what to say. Rusty stood up.

"Come on Mary, we're leaving."

Rusty was furious as we made our way to the front of the property. The van was waiting for us with the doors open. Another salesperson profusely apologized. We closed the door on them, and it was a relief to have the van take us back after that anxiety-producing seminar.

Samantha wasn't at the hotel when we returned. We wanted to let her know how forceful they had been. We hoped she was still going to come through with a judge on Saturday. Rusty and I opted for the pool and Jacuzzi over the beach that day. We needed to unwind from the stress of unrelenting selling tactics. The next morning, we caught Samantha at her booth in the middle of the lobby.

"Samantha, do you have any idea the high-pressure tactics those salesmen use?" Rusty asked.

"No, I didn't, but I will definitely be looking into it," she said, with worry in her eyes.

"Did you talk to your friend about marrying us tomorrow?" I asked.

"Oh, that's no problem, Mary. I have all the information written down here. She is expecting you tomorrow."

Samantha handed me a piece of paper with details on it. Rusty scanned the paper over my shoulder and looked satisfied. I let out a breath.

"What a relief. Thank you, Samantha. I can't believe our luck," I answered.

On Saturday, we woke up to a pure, blue sky and a dazzling sun. I put on my slim, white dress and matching hat. My hair was long and dark for the wedding pictures. My handsome husband wore a tuxedo. Samantha had come through with the delivery of a beautiful bouquet for me and a boutonniere for Rusty.

At ten o'clock, we walked out our door. There were already a dozen or so people in the lobby getting ready to start their day. A man and woman approached us. They asked if we were getting married. I smiled at them.

"Yes, we are. They're bringing our car around now," I beamed. The couple gasped.

"We're Beth and Ben Hartman and were from New York," Beth said, as she grasped my hand in hers.

"This is so exciting, right, Ben?"

Ben nodded. "Do you kids have your family here with you?" he asked.

Rusty chuckled. "Well, no."

I shrugged a little. "But we're happy doing this as just us."

Beth's eyes sparkled. "Sounds like a story and we've got time to listen. Don't we, Ben?"

Ben agreed, and encouraged by them, we shared our story. When we got to the part about this being our second wedding to each other, Beth leaned in close and said, "Sweetheart, don't mention that on this special day. Enjoy this day like it's your first. Treasure all the memories you are making today. This is your new beginning. The only important thing is now."

"Thank you, Beth. We'll do that," I said, as I looked over at my beaming, soon-to-be husband.

"You said you didn't have any family with you, right? Who's going to stand up for you and be your witnesses? You have to have someone with you," Beth frowned.

I shook my head. "The judge is supposed to take care of everything."

"You love birds need someone with you today," Ben said.

"We would love to go with you! Can we join you?" Beth asked.

Their bubbly, outgoing personalities were contagious. It made me even more excited than I already was.

"We don't want you to miss a day of your vacation on us," Rusty said.

Beth laughed. "Are you kidding? This will make an unbelievable story to tell when we get home. Do you think we're dressed all right?"

"Of course you are! You have no idea how much this means to us," I said, as I gave each one a big hug. The car rolled up to the front of the lobby. The four of us took off together as instant new friends.

"Well, it looks like a judge could live here," Rusty said. All four of us were taken in by the precise, manicured lawn, and the big, floor-to-ceiling windows.

"We're going to look ridiculous if it's the wrong house," I said, only half joking. We rang the doorbell. A uniformed maid with dark brown hair answered the door. Behind her, coming down the stairs, was a beautiful blonde in tennis whites.

"You must be Mary and Donald Bilger. I'm Judge Barbara Williams. For some reason, I was expecting a couple in shorts and tee shirts," she said, as she took in my white gown and Rusty's tuxedo. "You look wonderful. Are these two other people your parents?"

Before we could say no, Beth piped up. "Yes, we adopted them this morning!"

Judge Williams chuckled. "This is all so lovely. I'm going to run back upstairs and put something more appropriate on. Maria, please bring everyone something to drink."

We declined the drinks and sat in her beautiful, apparently professionally decorated home. Our heads turned every which way, trying to see everything. I didn't say it out loud, but I wondered how the woman trying to get customers to see timeshares was connected with this successful judge.

"I'm back," Judge Williams called, coming down the stairs. She was wearing a navy-blue pantsuit and heels. She was all smiles for us.

"I called and canceled my tennis match, so we don't have to rush. What do you think about having the ceremony out by the pool?"

I couldn't believe she was being so generous with her time. It felt like a dream. We followed her out of the sliding glass doors. She stood us in a spot that she thought would be conducive for pictures.

We said our "I Do's". Rusty put my original wedding ring back on my finger. The valuable twisty tie ring was tucked away in my jewelry box.

"Maria, please open a bottle of champagne so we may toast the new Mr. and Mrs. Bilger!" Judge Williams cheered. Beth and Ben clapped and hooted for us.

I couldn't have planned a more stunning wedding. And it was brought to us by none other than Samantha and her husband. I found out that they were the owners of the building that had the timeshares for sale. They were very good friends of Judge Barbara Williams. We got the best part of that deal.

"We're taking you out for a nice lunch and were not taking no for an answer," Beth said with a laugh after the ceremony.

"Rusty, find us a nice little restaurant, would you please?" Beth said, as Ben helped her into the back seat of our car. Over lunch they peppered us with questions.

"Well, at four we're leaving on a cruise to the Caribbean for a week. The day after we get back, Bob will fly into Orlando. We'll spend five days at Disney. I booked a room at the Contemporary Hotel, looking out at Cinderella's castle," I said.

"Oh, I am so happy for all of you. Let's eat up and go back to the hotel. And if it's ok with you, we will follow you to the pier in our car to see you off," Ben said.

"Mary, this is so exciting. I can't wait to tell all our friends that we got to be in a wedding!" Beth said. We laughed as we headed back to the hotel.

I could hear music and lots of chatter drifting through the lobby. Couples and groups passed the four of us by.

"What's going on?" I asked one of the staff members.

"Oh, on Saturdays, the hotel has a band that plays out by the pool. There's dancing and some refreshments. You should go and check it out. I'm sure everyone would love to see a bride and groom," The concierge smiled.

"Someone pinch me please," I said.

We walked out amid cheers and congratulations. This was their regular Saturday, but I accepted it as God's gift of a wedding reception for us. As fun as it was, we could only stay a short time.

Chapter 21

The cruise ship looked unbelievably huge to us. It towered over the low buildings on the edge of the boardwalk. A long shadow cast over us, blocking the bright, Miami sun. The name, "M. S. Boehme," was proudly displayed on the side in bold letters. We waited in a long line with our shipmates. They wanted to know if we had just gotten married or if the captain was marrying us on board. I had checked with the cruise line beforehand. They told me, "Our ship's Captain does not perform those duties, but we look forward to your arrival."

We booked a standard room with a port hole window. A kind person at guest services welcomed us as we checked in on board the ship. "Welcome Mr. and Mrs. Bilger, and congratulations on your big day! Since our Honeymoon Suite was not booked for this voyage, we were instructed to offer the Honeymoon Suite to you at no additional charge."

This news took my breath away. My feet were swept away too, as my husband picked me up to carry me to our room, with cheers echoing along the corridors from well-wishers. Rusty's muscles held out as he carried me over the threshold and into a very large cabin. He deposited both of us on the bed. Rusty panted and I laughed with a heart full of joy.

As my body soaked up the hot Caribbean sun, my mind drifted to who I was just a few years ago. I had been terribly unhappy. I zeroed in on what I thought my problems were. I craved having a life of my very own. I took the necessary steps to make it happen. It wasn't easy, and it came with a high price. A few people positively hated me.

To others, I was the mother who just walked out and left her husband and son, like I didn't care who was hurt in the process. A few others thought I was a nut case, leaving such a cushy life. My leaving to take care of my hurt soul was something I couldn't convey in words. I didn't know how to help others see it through my eyes. Not many men would have been so understanding. Not that Rusty was without fault, but he knew in his heart. He told me often.

"I know how much you love me and Bob. It's just a conflict between you and your past. You need to be your own best friend and work on yourself to understand what is going on. You have to make peace within."

That was exactly what I had spent the last year trying to do. A family life where we were all happy is what we both wanted. This time, we'd make it happen. My past did not define my present. But just as I determined this, my old family life crashed into my heart and mind again.

Rusty and I were back home. We'd been married for a few weeks. I received a telephone call, one pretty spring day, from my mother. That rotten S.O.B. Tom had finally done it. He'd hit the point of no redemption.

"Mary, Mary," my mother sobbed.

"Mom, I'm right here. Breathe," I said.

"Oh, Mary," Mom sobbed again.

That was all I could hear. She was crying so hard. Anxiety filled my mind, but I sounded as calm as I needed to be. I gently coaxed a few words out of her. Mom finally said something about a fight.

"Mary, they—the police took Tom away!" Mom cried.

My heart froze. "I'll be right there in 5 minutes," I hung up the phone.

I rushed to Rusty in the living room. He was watching TV. Bob was playing outside with some neighborhood kids. I told him it was my mom on the phone. She'd been crying.

"I didn't get much out of her but something's happened. I need you to watch Bob for me."

"All right. I'll be near the phone," he said.

I bolted out the door with my keys and purse. All of us lived on Chase Street, which was about ten to twelve blocks long. Mom lived at one end, and Rusty and I lived at the other end. Rusty's parents and grandparents owned houses in between us. When I arrived at Mom and Tom's house, people were milling around outside, talking in little groups.

From my car, I could already see the front windows were smashed out of their frames. But nothing could have prepared me for what I was about to see on the inside. I walked up the front porch steps. Broken glass was everywhere. It crunched under my shoes. I saw a man's white hanky soaked with red blood lying close to the front door. Spots of congealed blood were splattered inside. I prayed to God that Mom told me the truth. I had yelled into the phone earlier, *"Is everyone OK?"*

She answered, "Yes."

They were all in the living room when I entered. I gasped. My eyes took in the sight around me. I was overcome by the sheer destruction of everything in the room. The banister leading upstairs was torn apart. Part of it was used as a sledgehammer. The TV lay on its side, with the screen smashed in. Glass and debris were everywhere you stepped. Broken tables and lamps added to the bulk of destruction. It was hard to move around. I could see the dining room had not been spared either.

Dave, Ed, and Donna's school pictures lay on the floor with their pretty smiles looking up through the shattered glass. Broken crystal and plates were scattered around them. I was too numb to cry. My chest was tight. All I wanted were answers. I marched up to my family and hugged them, one by one. My mother's eyes were red.

Slowly, I was able to piece together what happened. I learned a little bit from everyone in the house. My heart ached for Donna. She was walking home from school. She saw the police put a bloody Tom into the police car.

"Mary, he was bleeding, and they just threw him in the car. But it was Ed that beat him up," Donna said in a horrified voice. Her eyes were wet.

Dave broke in, arms crossed defensively. "Ed was just trying to stop Tom."

"Will my dad be back Mary?" Donna asked.

I didn't answer her. I pulled Dave aside. "Start from the beginning. What the hell happened?" I said.

Dave had the most answers to how this warm, beautiful spring day had turned into a scene from a psychotic movie. He swallowed hard and looked me in the eyes.

"Mary, Tom was at the bar down on Galen Street all day. Mom asked me to walk down there and bring him home. He was really drunk and didn't want to go home. I stayed around for a while. He told me to go on home and tell Mom he would be along shortly. It was probably another hour before he got here. He no sooner walked in the door when they started fighting. We had the record player going and that made Tom upset, so he picked it up with both hands. He pulled the cord out of the wall and threw it across the room. Then Tom stood there and broke all our records. He was yelling and cussing and breaking everything he could get his hands on."

Dave told me it was Ed that got control over Tom. I looked over at Ed, who was rumpled and sweaty, but he didn't have a scratch on him. Ed was going on seventeen and could take care of himself. He had been working out a lot. Dave had also hit his teen years, but Donna was just seven.

Ed walked over to me, grim-faced. "I just couldn't take it anymore. I'm so tired of living like this, Mary."

I knew what he meant. Ed became our hero that day, but I'm sure Mom didn't feel that way. Mom realized she had to have Tom arrested. Because if she didn't, Ed would. Ed had accomplished more in one afternoon than I had in a lifetime. I was proud of the boys, and so thankful everyone was safe. But I couldn't stand to even look at our mother. In my eyes, this was all her fault. My brothers and sister had paid the price. Ed got Tom out of the house that day, but I wanted him far, far away. I wanted Tom out of our lives forever. I would do whatever it took to make that happen.

I started by keeping track of Tom's court case. The day he got out of jail I knew he would head straight to Mom to try and kiss and make up. That was what he always did. He knew where he could find her, which was at the hospital. The month before, she made arrangements to go into the hospital for some tests and a small procedure on her foot. I don't know where I got the guts to do what I did next. I made a call to the hospital pretending to be someone from the courthouse.

"Yes, I'm here to inform you that Christine Falkenburg's significant other was just released. We have it on file that he mentioned finding her here at this hospital. There is reason to believe that the two of them should not make contact, due to the nature of this case."

The hospital receptionist put me on hold for a few minutes which felt like an eternity.

"Ma'am, what we can do is put a 'no visitors allowed' sign on her door and keep a very close watch on her."

I let out the breath I had been holding. "Thank you, I'll follow up with the court."

I hung up the phone. I allowed myself a moment to bask in my success. I took a deep breath. I put my next call to my mother. I told her what I had done. Mom was stunned.

"So, he can't come to see me here? What if he wants to—"

"Don't go to him. Don't let him come near you, even if you get out of the hospital early."

"Mary," she said.

"Mom, if you so much at say 'Hi' to that man again, you will lose every one of us."

And I wasn't kidding. The tone of my voice left no room for argument or doubt.

On the day that Tom was to appear before the judge for his charges, my mother didn't appear in court. Rusty was working, so I went by myself to represent my past, my family, and my wounded heart. Someone was going to listen to me today. They were going to hear more than Tom's version of the truth. I heard he had a good lawyer. I was afraid they would just let him go. I went to the courthouse and found out where I needed to be. I walked down the beige hallway and into a waiting room that had chairs and tables set up to provide a little privacy.

As soon as I entered, I locked eyes with Tom. He looked shocked to see me. He leaned over and started talking to the guy sitting next to him, which I assumed was a lawyer. He looked like a lawyer – he had on a suit, tie, white shirt, and dark dress shoes. They had their heads bent together for a long time, whispering. I took a seat across from them.

His lawyer got up and walked out of the room. I didn't feel afraid to sit there and stare at Tom across the room. I felt determined. Tom averted his eyes. The ceiling light was bright, but there wasn't anything interesting to look at, just a clock on the far wall. The lawyer wasn't gone long. He was in deep conversation with Tom again. I wasn't close enough to hear anything. A few minutes later, a man walked into the room and straight over to me.

"Hello, Mary Bilger? My name is David Morgan. Could I speak with you for a minute?"

"Absolutely, sir. Nice to meet you."

I stood and shook his hand. Mr. Morgan said his office was just across the hall. I agreed to go with him. I sat in a leather chair across from his desk. Mr. Morgan opened a file.

"I understand that you're here to represent your mother today. I would like to hear your side of the story."

I swallowed. "All right," I agreed.

With every bit of raw emotion I had in me, I unloaded all the abuse, fear, and hurt all of us endured for years. I was shaking when I was done. Mr. Morgan looked at me with what I thought was compassion. I hoped he believed me. With a smile and no words, he placed a few phone calls from the telephone on his desk. I took out a handkerchief from my purse and focused on my breathing. It sounded like Mr. Morgan was looking for someone over the phone. Then, before he could say anything, he had an incoming call. I stopped wiping my eyes.

My God, it dawned on me. This guy could be working with Tom's attorney. *Oh no, what have I done?* I thought. My heart lost a beat. I forgot to breathe.

The first words that came out of this man's mouth were, "Tom should rot in hell for what he has done to this family. Let this young lady have her day in court. He's nothing but a mean drunk, Jim."

They continued talking, but my brain had stopped listening. *He believed me. I can't believe this person wants to help me.*

I felt like I was going to float away, I was so happy.

When I returned to the hearing room, Tom wouldn't look in my direction. It wasn't long before we were all seated at a big table in another room. Tom and his lawyer were on one side. I was on the other. The man at the end of the table was the judge. When it was my turn to speak, the judge looked at me.

"Take your time Mrs. Bilger. There's no need to be nervous."

"Yes, your Honor," I said quietly.

I should have kept my shaking hands in my lap, I guess. Maybe they could all see it. I took a deep breath. I repeated the story for the judge. He listened and took notes. Tom's lawyer sat next to him. The judge folded his hands on top of the table.

"Well Mr. Roach, you're a drunk," the judge said.

"No Sir. I drink, but I'm not an alcoholic," Tom answered.

The judge was starting to answer Tom back when Tom interrupted the judge. Tom's attorney broke into the conversation immediately.

"Tom, the judge is trying to help you. Pay attention to what he's saying."

Tom scowled darkly. I knew he was done for. That judge was going to make him pay. This was the end of Tom. The judge said he had to make restitution. Tom had to attend some classes. He had to report to someone on a regular basis. I knew he would never do any of those things. Tom would skip town. And he did. My family and I never saw him again. Just like that, the reign of Tom was finally over. All that was left, was for my family to pick up the pieces of our hearts, from the broken years.

Chapter 22

We had a new home built not long after the reign of Tom ended. We wanted Bob to be in a better school system, and our little doll house was becoming too small for us. We moved to Shoreland. It had a Toledo mailing address, but it was not annexed and never would be because of how the laws were drawn up. Shoreland had its own school system, police, and fire department. It was a great neighborhood. My siblings and I were all married couples with kids now. The neighborhood kids were always out playing in the evenings. Parents got together in our yard or another.

Several years after moving to Shoreland, we had some friends from across the street come over to our house in the evening. Their names were Roger and pat Combs. They were a nice couple with two younger boys.

"Did we mention to you about the seminar we went to recently? It was a three-day class," Roger said. He opened his beer and took a sip.

"Why are you guys attending a motivational class?" I blurted.

"Because they work," Pat said simply. "It's helped our communication with each other, and in understanding ourselves. The both of us learned how to get rid of the crap that kept us from being happy."

"Well, if someone can make me feel happier, sign me up," I laughed. "What do you think Rusty?"

Rusty shrugged. "If you want to do it, go for it. There's no way I have time for something like that."

"Yeah, I think I am interested. When and where is the next seminar?" I said. I put a handful of Jiffy Pop popcorn in my mouth.

I attended the next "People Synergistically Involved" or PSI seminar. It was being held in one of the bigger hotels in downtown Toledo. The class was small; I was one of 25 students in the conference room. The speakers handed out assignments for us to participate in. Most of the class was discussion-based, to allow us to get involved. There wasn't any material given to us at the time, but I took rigorous notes. I was in the right place at the right time. The knowledge that the speakers shared started me on a path that I would travel on for the rest of my life. It opened up something in me, aspects of my life that I never question before. It was hard and fun at the same time.

To say that it changed my life is an understatement. I was just like Roger and Pat when they tried to describe it to us. I wanted to understand how my mind worked. I wanted to understand how life worked. But most importantly, I wanted to heal. I could tell these for my first baby steps to the true healing of myself.

For me, the class made me understand the power of my mind and how it worked within the "Laws of Life" to bring me peace. The "Universal Laws of Life" pertain to how life itself works on a conscious and subconscious level. It is a set of ideas that have been explored by more than one author. It was different from the laws of natural science I studied as a girl. But that didn't mean it was no less real. I couldn't see sound waves, but I knew they exist. Soundwaves allow me to listen to music on the radio in the kitchen. In the same way, studying the universal laws helped me to understand how everything works in harmony in life.

I was under the impression that things just "happened" to me in life. Everything was just meant to be as if it was sent by God. But the PSI class made me realize that this "divine power" resided in me. It could hear my every thought, not just the words that came after "Heavenly Father," in my prayers. I had a responsibility to think positively. I can't tell you how many times I said, "I'm so messed up", "I hate that", or "I can't do it." That was how I lived my whole life, growing up in the home environment I had.

Now I was awakened to some very profound, new understanding. Divine power was active and working in my life through the universal laws I learned. I had a responsibility in what I said, because the divine listened to all my dialog, trying to give me what I was saying. If I thought badly about myself, if I spoke badly about myself, I would believe in what I was saying. I would reap what I sowed because that is how a law, a truth, worked. I understood this now. I practiced in order to help turn my life around in my thinking. I became aware of what I was saying and thinking. It was powerful. It was hard. But I could do it.

I started seeing and feeling the difference in my life. I became aware of my oneness with God and what that meant. The universal law of divine oneness was active in my life, and I was wholeheartedly participating in this work myself.

I recognized bad habits that I picked up during the time I had a "Mary" life. I used to go dancing or socialize after work, and from there, I picked up smoking and drinking. Back then, I didn't care. I was having fun, trying to give my soul the freedom she craved. But now I recognized these habits as self-destructive to my body and my mind. I decided to quit smoking and drinking. I started to look better than I had in years. I was kinder, more giving, and more understanding of myself and others. But there were still problems in my marriage.

Why am I unhappy in my marriage?

I asked myself this over and over. Was it my emotional baggage? I made it a point of facing my demons. I harbored anger towards my father for years, but I never acknowledged it. I found forgiveness in my heart for him, along with understanding. December 14, 1959. That was one painful memory I unearthed from the closet in the back of my mind. I embraced the hurt, the anger, and the shock from the deepest part of my soul. I learned to let it go. I had so much more to unburden.

My heart was full of resentment towards my mother. I had to forgive her in my heart, too. This took a great deal of work. I realized that given the circumstances she was living in at the time, my mom did the best she could. In the years after Tom left both of our lives for good, Mom raised my siblings on her own. I helped where I could, even to help raise Donna until she moved. In a few years when my siblings were growing into their own lives, Mom moved in with Rusty, Bob, and me.

At first, Mom and I kept the living arrangement kind, on a surface level. She had her life, and I had mine with my family. But in a little while, things changed. After dinner one night, I put away the roast beef. Mom grabbed the plates off the table.

"You go ahead and watch some TV with Rusty. I'll take care of this," Mom said.

"Are you sure, Mom?" I asked.

"Of course. You worked all day, didn't you? Go relax," she smiled.

I couldn't believe it. For the first time I'd seen in years, Mom took care of the dishes. She started helping with the laundry, too. Mom even put off time from hanging out with her friends to spend time with me, or watch Bob. It was like the things that happened when I was just a little girl, were reversed. Mom and I started talking more. We had better conversations. I worked on our relationship. I worked on my feelings until we had a true, loving bond. I was still working on my hatred towards Tom.

My mind did not want to give that one up. I wrote down all the incidents that I could think of. All the hurts that I felt he was responsible for in my life. I tried my best to rid myself of the hate I hadn't been able to express. As I was writing, I felt each incident. I took a deep breath while I sat on my bed. A pad of paper and pencil was in my hand. The lined page was blank.

I remembered the way he struck me across the face when Mom was in the hospital. I could hear the sound. I could feel the sting on my cheek all over again, the hot rage in my heart. I wrote it down. I exhaled. I reminded myself that Tom was gone.

I hate you, but my hatred is only hurting me, not you.

"I am choosing to let that go," I whispered. I wrote each word. Anytime my mind brought the memory, or the thought up I replaced it. "*I am choosing to let that go*". Every time I remembered some horrible thing Tom did, I wrote it down. I felt it. I let it go, again and again.

It seemed like my hatred for Tom was always on my mind. Even though it was true, it didn't make it right to keep carrying that hatred in my heart. If I kept holding onto this, I would just be drinking my poison, rotting my soul. I needed to face my emotional baggage. It felt like I was straining against old, huge, and ugly suitcases stuck in the closet in my mind. I undid the metal clasps. I pulled out the content that needed to go. I needed to replace the bad feelings in my heart. I was striving for something new, something "good". I knew it would eventually come.

My father, my mom, and Tom. I had done as much as I could in my own heart. But what about my marriage? What was the truth about my marriage that I've never faced? Something was still causing me problems in that area of my life.

Around this time, there was a family vacation that Rusty and I had planned to go on with Bob. We had been looking forward to this for three long months while Bob was in school. The three of us were going away for a small vacation. Bob and I were looking forward to this. We were going to stay at a beachside resort in Florida. I started packing our things for the trip in one of our spare bedrooms. I had a "To-Do" list a couple of pages long. I was a big believer in the "Five P's Plan" – Proper Planning Prevents Piss Poor Results.

I finally had everything on my list checked off, and I found someone to take care of our mail for us. The only thing left was to find some good books to take with me. The day before we were supposed to leave, Rusty came home from work, looking a little sheepish.

"Rusty are you okay, you look a little funny," I asked. I was stirring spaghetti sauce on the stove. Bob and Rusty loved the way I made the sauce. Rusty gently took my elbow.

"Mary, come sit down. I have something I need to tell you."

The both of us sat at the table. I took a sip of Pepsi and held the ice-cold glass to calm my nerves.

"Honey, what's going on?" I asked. Worry entered my heart. He took his time before he finally answered me.

"Sweetheart, I'm sorry, but we can't go on vacation tomorrow."

"What the hell are you talking about?" I yelled.

I think I had a little inkling about what he was going to say from the moment he told me to sit down, but I wasn't ready to hear it. Not after all that work I put in for this trip.

"There's a huge project starting, and I have to work on it."

I didn't give Rusty time to say another word.

"You have to work, or you *want* to work? No, you know what? Don't even bother trying to answer that. I know what the answer is already."

"Mary, they want me to work as a General Foreman, and you know how much that pays. It would be foolish to turn it down."

I wanted to throw my glass of Pepsi in his calm, smirking face as he sat there taking off his dirty boots on my clean, kitchen floor. I stood up and turned off the stove. I walked away with my Pepsi. The next day he started his project.

I couldn't believe he'd done this at the last possible minute. I managed to cancel everything so that he could work. Instead of spending time together in the sun on a beach, we were stuck in Ohio. I took care of Bob after school and the house. Rusty worked out of town for the next two months. This wasn't the first time his work took him out of the way, and far from us. It hit me one night, alone in my bed.

When I faced my truth, I realized how extremely *lonely* I felt in my marriage. I talked to Rusty about him working so much. I told him that I needed him home with me more. He had a work ethic that would not let him walk away from any over time. The union hall could provide him with new jobs constantly. He was very much in demand because of the quality of his work and his love for making money. Rusty was always trying to top his last paycheck. But he wasn't home as much as I wanted him to be.

There were months when we would see each other for less than an hour a day. I'd be going to work, and he'd be coming home from work. There were months when he would work out of town. It was a double-edged sword. I couldn't fault him for wanting to provide for his family, but the fact was, it made me feel abandoned, unhappy, and lonely. I talked to Rusty several times about it, but it seemed he couldn't change himself any more than I could change how I felt.

I started going out more and more without him. It got to a point where we were living different lives. I left before and I wasn't happy, so what would I gain by leaving again? I didn't know, but divorce number two was happening regardless.

Chapter 23

This time I took my son with me and got an apartment. I knew I couldn't make it without Bob. I didn't want him to change schools, so I would drive him there in the mornings and he could take the bus back to our old house. His dad was still living there, which I was happy about. That made it better for Bob. But it didn't take me long to understand how unhappy my son was.

He went outside to play one day after we got home from school and work. As I was making dinner, I looked out the window and watched him. He was just a little boy, standing outside by himself, looking around. There were no friends for him to play with. Tears welled in my eyes. Yes, it had made me happy having him with me, but not at this cost. It broke my heart, but I took Bob back to his dad, to Rusty.

I had to do some soul searching after Bob left. I kept a diary of some sort over the years since the PSI class, to write down my thoughts and to unburden my heart. I read the diaries again. In my heart, I had always taken one-hundred percent responsibility for our divorces. At the same time, I knew with certainty that I loved Rusty and always had. So I spent the next several months trying to figure out some underlying causes. I wanted to try and figure out what was going on in our relationship. We were still seeing each other regularly. As a matter of fact, we were spending more time together than when I lived with him. What was going on?

One day, I came across a page in my diary that hit me with a jolt. I sat on my bed. The apartment was quiet after work. The sky was painted in fiery oranges, yellows, and passionate red. The last light of the sun filtered through my window and illuminated the words on the page. My hands shook as I read what I had written before.

I wrote, *"I have to get my feelings out, at least on paper, since I can't talk to you Rusty. We can't even stand to be around each other anymore. I thought you going on the night shift might help, but it only made things worse. Throughout this whole marriage, you have always said you can't tell me anything. I don't listen to you, and nothing is my fault. Did you ever stop and think those words apply to you also?*

To be honest with you, I was glad that you were gone on your long work project. I felt relief that you were gone. Just think about the things that you have flown off the handle about recently. I went to the store on the way home from work to get some groceries. I came home later than I planned, and you got mad at me. Did I ever yell at you about coming home late from work?

Remember when I watched television instead of being in the kitchen when you and Bob were eating? It was hard watching you guys eat when I was trying to lose some weight. And you got mad at me for that too, after I told you why I wasn't at the table. I'm tired of arguing with you, Rusty. Our lives have become like two ships passing in the night.

The funny thing about all of this is that I used to run around half the night before our first divorce, and you treated me like gold! The worse I treated you, the better you treated me. That has been the dance we've been doing all these years. Just think about it. When we were first married, you treated me shitty. You went out for drinks with your work friends. It didn't matter if I needed help at home with the baby. You still went. You didn't want to spend time with me and our friends. You even thought you made a mistake marrying me! You admitted this to me so don't try and deny it now.

Did you think I didn't know how you really felt? But when I thought I had to get out of the marriage and didn't want to be married to you, it was like magic.

You were so in love with me again. I was something to be treasured instead of being treated like a mistake. And we did that dance again. I hope you acknowledge your part in all of this. Please don't come up with petty little excuses. I wrote these things out before, but I never gave them to you. The fact that I am now, well, I am not doing this dance anymore."

I never gave Rusty my writings. I told myself, again, what a wonderful husband he was. He was a man who worked hard to provide for his family. But I was lonely in our marriage. We weren't communicating. But uncovering this now with fresh eyes and a better understanding, I knew this was part of the problem. It made me think back.

I realized Rusty treated me the same way he treated his cars. He had an old, black, clunker of a car. The best thing you could say about it was that it ran most of the time. Rusty loved that car. He didn't have to worry about where he parked it so it wouldn't get dings on the doors. He had the freedom to just enjoy it. But only because he had a beautiful, new car covered up in his grandmother's garage. Rusty rarely took the newer car out for a ride. In the same way, that's how I felt about how he treated me in our marriage. For Rusty, his work was a lot like the old, clunky black car. His work was what he pursued the most in his life, his drive. But in our marriage, I was not given the attention that I needed. I felt like the newer car he had, just waiting to be taken out for a drive at least once in a while.

There were times when Rusty would enjoy going to "Geneva on the Lake," to work. This was a place where some of his long-term, good-paying jobs were at Perry Nuclear Power House. It was also a great fishing spot. Month after month Rusty stayed there. Several of his best working buddies were with him. He told me about all the fun he was having going out to eat with them and going fishing. Rusty could do this because he was working nights. And I was left at home, missing him, feeling lonely in our marriage again.

His good car didn't care if he was gone for months, but his wife sure did. The dance of our life was staring me in the face after I read my confession. I had to get up and do something while my thoughts spun and my heart filled with realization. I started baking a cake for myself. I opened the fridge and sighed.

What a pair Rusty and I were. I don't think there was another couple more in love than the two of us. Nor was there a couple with more problems. No one could understand our relationship. My mother knew we were meant to be, but his family didn't always understand. We didn't care. Rusty and I always felt love and care that pumped beneath the avalanche of our problems. I knew that would always be true. So after the cake was made, I decided to visit Rusty. I waited for Rusty to get home. We shared a cold drink and talked about our days and how Bob was doing. That was good. Now time for the hard part. I took a deep breath.

"Rusty, do you think this is okay between us? Because I don't think we can keep doing this back-and-forth dance."

I pulled my journal from my purse. I read what I had written, the words I never had the nerve to give him before. Now as I read it, he sat in his chair, stunned. I could tell he was in deep thought, but I felt no anger coming from him. I didn't have any anger when I approached this conversation and read my words. I read my letter to him, and he stayed seated.

"Mary, I couldn't agree more. My God, I love you so much. I want this to work. It has to work. When you're not here it feels like something's missing. But even if we got back together, what happens if we just go in circles again?"

"I know, and I don't want that to happen either. But I also want to know what you feel and what you think."

We made up our minds to keep digging until we flushed out everything about ourselves that could be contributing to our yo-yo life, this back-and-forth dance, together. Like building a house or any good kind of cake, it was always best to start with good products.

During the last few years, I worked hard to acknowledge the feelings that I had tucked away so long ago. I became aware that when I felt threatened or hurt, my feelings completely turned off. I went into defense mode. I operated this way since I was a child. I had the same reaction to a small problem in my life, such as someone saying something that hurt my feelings, as I had when it came to hurtful, traumatic events. I shut down, and my little girl handed me the response I couldn't even think of at the moment.

I always pushed my true feelings and thoughts to the back of my mind. It was automatic unless what I was feeling in the present was extremely painful, such as when I went into labor as a teen and as a young adult.

I was still disconnecting from the present, even as an adult. I was hiding my true feelings and thoughts. I had to figure this out. I couldn't keep living this way. I had to pay attention to myself in a different way. I learned to be very conscious of my thoughts and what physical reactions were taking place in my body. My first reactions were the same. I became numb the moment I felt threatened or hurt. Now I was aware of when this happened. I could choose how I wanted to respond, at least most of the time.

Another thing Rusty and I learned was our communication was just surface level talking. We stated our problems and waited for the other person to make the necessary change to fix them. We started with the work problem. Many women would not have a problem with their husbands being gone all the time. I did. I also realized I had a right to my feelings even though he brought home a big paycheck. I also understood that Rusty had a right to his feelings and beliefs also. He opened up to me while the two of us strolled through the park, just for a change of pace. The shadows from the trees drifted over our clothes. Gravel crunched underneath our feet.

"Mary, I was brought up with a strong work ethic. Work came first. Dad was my example. I remember as a young kid, I couldn't wait for summer to come so I could make some money. Don't get me wrong, dad provided for all our needs. We weren't rich, but we had everything we needed. I just wanted to make my own money."

"I can understand that, but to cancel a family vacation the night before we were going to leave is a little bit extreme, don't you think? We have to come up with some kind of balance."

Rusty rubbed the back of his neck. I reached for his hand.

"I understand the drive that you have, and where it comes from, but I'm entitled to have my feelings acknowledged, and the biggest one is loneliness. Experience has taught me that I hate spending so much time alone. Now that I'm aware of this, I'll try and control my super sensitivity to this problem. But we have to meet in the middle, Rusty."

Rusty squeezed my hand as we walked. "I'll do this, Mary; whenever you feel lonely from me being gone so much, I promise that I'll work with you. Just let me know when you start to feel lonely."

I smiled at him. "Thank you, honey. I want us to work this out so badly. I think this just might do it!"

He followed through with his promise. When he took on a long-term job, he checked on me. Like for North Star Steel, which was an eight-month project which had him working seven days a week. On most days Rusty worked ten to thirteen hours on that project. Rusty always made sure I was doing okay at those times, and I was. I laughed with him over the phone once during one of his check-ins with me.

"You remind me of the Energizer bunny—you just keep going and going!"

Rusty was in his element now, and he was happy at home too. It was a win-win for us at last. A simple conversation with no blame and no demands had gotten us over a big hurdle.

We had arrived at a balance. His tendency to overwork became a "non-issue" with us. Deep communication had worked. We got over our egos, and all attention was placed on solutions. That is when I started seeing good results in my life.

In the past, I'd wanted to solve a problem, but all I did was re-hash the problem from different viewpoints. Now, I didn't just think about a problem. I laid it out on paper, using words that kept my focus on what I wanted the result to be.

Chapter 24

No one would have believed that our relationship could reach the loving heights that it did after two divorces. But as the years racked up and Bob finished middle school and then high school, the non-believers started asking what our secret was. Our results spoke for us.

More than anything else, I wanted a happy family life. The same was true for Rusty. That was our starting point. We knew we loved each other. I, more than Rusty, believed in a power that was omnipresent and could be accessed to help in any situation. Anyone can define and label this aspect of life and the universe differently, but this is my interpretation of it. For me this power is divine. My understanding of it indeed began in a church setting, but the divine working in my life was not limited to Sunday sermons and prayers.

First, this divine power acted in my life on its own to keep my sanity from slipping away since I was a little girl. The divine was there in that dark place during labor, and the divine was there when I first needed to scream after seeing my father. And now, I learned to access my connection to divine power over the years to help learn my truth.

This was in part through the use of my brain and mind, not just my spirit. I do not believe my brain and mind are the same. I believe my brain is my physical learning tool. But I believe that my mind is connected to my soul, and connected to divine power working intrinsically in my life. Whatever I learned from my brain has a deep effect on my mind and my soul.

I learned that this could affect everything about me and how I operate in the world. I have learned good things and I have learned disturbing things, such as the idea that my father killed himself because of me. I believed that as a girl. I believed that I was no more than unwanted crabgrass as a teenager. These were bad thoughts in my brain that I unconsciously put into place. They had affected every area of my life and mind.

I believed them to be true, so they were. That was my brain running my life. So if my brain was running my life based on whatever information it experienced, whether true or not, why couldn't I flood my brain with good thoughts and experience good things?

But where was God in all of this? I had experienced that presence of divine power enough times to know that it existed. But that knowing, couldn't, wouldn't, and didn't, stop me from going down some wrong paths. So what was going on here? I thought about this often while at work. When I went home, I would write down my thoughts in my diary. I went to the bathroom, my place of refuge, and thought about it while setting up a bath. My diary was open from where I left off with this question. I pillowed my head on my arm over the side of the tub. I stared at the question mark at the end of that sentence. *Where was God in all this?*

Obviously, I had free choice. I made choices on what I believed to be true about myself. I did that as much as I could, for my whole life. The feelings from those thoughts unconsciously dictated my actions, and therefore my life choices. But could I make myself a better person by flooding my life with deliberate positive thoughts and ideas? And if I did that, would I essentially be saying "Thanks God, but I'll take over now"?

I realized that the way I thought of myself was a lot like how to make soup for dinner. My soul was made up of whatever ingredients I put into my life based on my feelings and my thoughts. Letting those thoughts marinate and boil over time would produce the flavor of my soul, the aroma of my soup. Since I was young I added bad ingredients, bad thoughts and feelings, to my soul soup. Now I needed to start over. I needed to make a better soup out of my life and my heart. I got out of the bath to dry off quickly. I picked up my pen. Droplets splashed on my diary, but I needed to write this down.

My first new ingredient was self-power. I was learning what to do with positive thinking, new knowledge, self-reflection, and love. All of these felt so good to have in my life now. But there was still more to my soul's ingredients, and I was just discovering the depth of them.

How could I make my soul soup from all the ingredients God let me taste? I wanted to make a damn good soup. The flavor would be in the results, and I was starving for a better soup than what I had for most of my life.

My quest for more understanding started with Thomas's writings and seminars in 1977, at the same time as the PSI class I took. His teaching touched my soul and opened my eyes to my connection to the world. But knowing something and living something are two very different things. After my bath, I grabbed a book from my nightstand. I flipped open the thin pages on my bed. It was the King James version of the Bible. The opening chapter of the Gospel of John reads,

"In the beginning was the Word,
and the Word was with God, and the Word was God."
- John 1:1 (King James Version, KJV)

That was the most powerful sentence I had ever read. That one sentence resonated with me and never went away. I started paying attention to all the words that came out of my mouth. How important were the words I spoke? Could that really make a difference in my life? I began with the assumption that this was a true statement. Everything started with words.

I started being careful with what I said. I made a conscious choice to be as positive as I could in my mind. That was really hard to do. I didn't realize how much I talked without thinking. It takes practice and practice to be conscious of every thought and to slow them down enough to examine them before you allow words to escape from your mouth. I realized that the words I speak influence my thoughts and vice versa. My words can impact how I feel and how I think about myself, others, and the world around me.

Words are thoughts. My positive thoughts did start to produce some very good results in my life. I realized that I wasn't crabgrass. I was a budding flower, stretching for the sun. I was different from the others. I was different from the other girls that I went to high school with because of my experiences and the way my mind worked. And that was okay.

When it came to my father, I realized that what he did was his own decision. The root of blaming myself was out of my anger, because of how his decision impacted me and my family. Once I change my perspective on these very hurtful and damaging ideas, my soul soup improved. The aroma was becoming better. It was mouth-watering.

My life was better than before. The first thing I noticed was how buoyant I felt. It took me a while to string enough happy days together to realize my life was running smoothly--much more smoothly. Before long I had a real "Ah- ha!" moment, a moment where I truly realized it wasn't a coincidence that my life was changing for the better. I was making it happen.

I was driving my car the day after a bad snowstorm in Toledo. I hit a patch of black ice. My car started to spin around. My car crossed over into the oncoming traffic lane. I slid into a snowdrift. My seatbelt caught me. My first reaction was fear, but that only lasted a second. My mind took over with my new programming.

"Everything will be fine! Everything will be fine!" I yelled.

I said it out loud over and over until my car came to a stop in the snowdrift. My hands shook at the wheel. I took several shallow breaths. I felt giddy with relief. I worked with my car. I tried to get traction going back and forth, but I couldn't get the car out. I was stuck. I was going to have to get pulled out. Someone knocked on the glass.

"Ma'am can I help you?" came a voice on the other side of my window.

I let out a relieved breath. "Yes, thank you!" I said.

I never questioned coincidence again. I was happy. My appetite for more understanding just kept growing stronger. I read more books. I read "Power Through Constructive Thinking" by Emmett Fox, first published in 1932, and "Riches Within Your Reach" by Robert Collier, first published in 1947, that winter. I devoured every word. The one thing they all had in common was a belief in a higher power. There was energy floating around in my head, covering all my thoughts. I learned to slow down my thinking and become aware of how things came together. I wanted to know why everyone wasn't using this gift of self-knowledge, awareness, and self-power. Instead of just reading these concepts, I started living them out in my life through continuous practice and prayer.

In my brain, to reach God I bowed my head and asked God to help. And many, many times, I received. I knew that worked. But as I started to study more, I realized that was only the little tip of the iceberg. A whole mountain of his divine power was waiting for me. But knowing something and living something were two very different things. What did I have to do differently?

I didn't know exactly how it worked. I wasn't given this divine power. I became aware of it and made an active decision to learn how to access it. I proved to myself the existence of divine power in my life with results. This was just another ingredient to my soul soup, one that was always on the counter but hardly ever used with effective practice. Now, I was armed with knowledge from the Bible, Thomas Willhite, Emmett Fox, and Robert Collier. But reading was just the first step of my soul soup project.

Knowledge tended to drift away into forgetfulness. The next thing I did was put my desires in written form. I made a long-term goal board and divided it into four sections. I learned this from Mr. Willhite's teachings. Health, Wealth, Love, and My Expressions were the four areas that I needed to balance in my life. I didn't have a white construction board, so I used the top of a white gift box. I was so excited about making this thing. It felt like I was in a store, putting my order in.

I spent a Saturday working on this project. I took off a white box top from my closet. I cut each corner of the box top with a pair of scissors so that I could lay it flat on my desk. With a black marker, I divided each of the four sections and labeled them with headings in capital letters. I flipped through several magazines. I cut out pictures to visualize what I wanted. I would add notes over time, I knew that. So I planned to leave space in each section.

I sat back with a soft smile on my face. The beginning of my goal board stared back at me from under the glow of the lamp on my desk. I spent a lot of time thinking about what changes would enrich my life. I couldn't wait to get started.

Chapter 25

I started to be kinder to myself. I would stop talking in mid-sentence if I was putting myself down. That was a hard one to try and change but now I could honestly feel my goodness and love for others. My husband and son made a point of parking the car in front of Jacobson's. It was the nicest store in our mall. They did that because I had said, "I can't shop here, this store is for rich people."

Rusty stopped me right in front of their jewelry department. He looked at me.

"Mary, there isn't a thing in this store you can't afford. The jewelry, the furs upstairs—you could walk out the door *today* with anything you wanted. You have the mentality that you don't deserve these things, but you do deserve it."

He was right. I bought myself a beautiful bracelet that day.

"Thank you for your observation, my dear husband. I think I'm going to like learning this lesson," I chuckled.

The Wealth section became easy to fill in. I found a picture of bundles of hundred-dollar bills and a women's hand holding them. I cut that out from the magazine and pasted it to the goal board. Using a red pen I painted her nails bright red, just like mine. I wrote my name on all the bundles. Using a black marker, I drew dollar signs in the Wealth section. I wrote underneath the picture, *"RICH is having money that you don't have a purpose for. I am Rich."*

That felt so good to write, and it was even better when I started experiencing the start of true wealth a short time later. I was fortunate to pick up a job where I could work for a Fortune 500 company. I used my paycheck to pay off our larger bills. I also started putting more money into savings. It felt good to define a purpose for money. We weren't at my definition of wealth yet, but little by little I knew we could get there.

Love was the next section to work on for my goal board. I wrote the word "Love" in the upper portion of the board and underlined it. Right under that I wrote in bold black, *"To Give Love and to Feel Loved."* For me, this was about self-love first. If I couldn't feel love for myself, how could I feel love for someone else the way I wanted to? If I could feel better about myself as a person, I knew that I could truly care about others from a genuine place of love. I wanted to show other people in my life that connection through my words and actions.

I started treating myself as worthy of all the good life had to offer. When I discovered this, it became easy to extend the same to others. I was worthy of forgiveness for myself. It became so much easier to see why people behaved the way they did. When I understood this, it opened the door to forgiveness for others. Forgiveness for me was a huge mountain of untapped potential just waiting to be used. And this was how I did it. Forgiving myself had to come first before I could treat myself or others the worth they deserved.

The Health portion of my goal board was overflowing with ideas. At the top, I wrote the names of my loved ones. *"Rusty, Bob, Mom, Dad, my mom, Donna, Ed, and Dave,"* and others. I wanted all of them to live long, happy, healthy lives. For myself, I wrote in a bright red pen, *"I Am Accepting of Myself," "Continuous Energy", "Live in Grace",* and *"The Older I Get, the Better I Look."*

I summed it all up on a new line. *"In a Nutshell, I want peace, happiness, and to look really good."* I wasn't sure how I was going to accomplish these health goals yet. But just having the thought first and writing it down was the start of being able to manifest the goal for my life. I knew it would all come together. I looked out my window and saw three girls riding their bikes down the street. I used to love playing outside and swimming when I was younger. Maybe I could make play a form of exercise. Exercise was always talked about in TV commercials, but maybe it didn't have to be this big, grueling thing. If I at least picked up a little bike riding, that couldn't hurt to try. And from there, I started to think that I could plan at least one healthy meal a week.

The last fourth of my board was dedicated to My Expressions. In big, bold, black lettering with a blue trim around each word, I wrote, *"REALIZATION OF GOD"*. I had taken the first page out of my copy of "Power Through Constructive Thinking". I taped it to my board. I wanted to always remember the important part of what personal self-expression meant to me.

When I finished setting up my goals and looked at my board, I felt happiness and anxiousness for results. I anticipated all of this happening in my life in some way, somehow. This was just the start. I wanted to learn how to accomplish my goals. I thumbed through titles in the library. I studied more books that focused on self-reflection, and ideas that focused on the universal laws of life. I didn't just read the books; I dissected each paragraph. I wanted to make sure I understood the truth they were trying to convey and how my thinking and life matched up or not. I kept my Goal Board under my bed, along with my daily writings.

My writing included observations of how things were working in my life. I wrote down my feelings and thoughts about my daily life. I wrote and studied whenever I had the time. If I had a day off and Bob was in school, I made the most of that time. If Rusty worked out of town, I made use of the time I had. Whatever time I could have outside my life as a wife, mother, and company worker, I used it for myself.

I would take everything out to keep my ideas alive. I would put my writings and books back in their hiding spots when I was done. I didn't want to leave them out so others could tell me that I was crazy and it was a stupid idea. I didn't want to chance outside interference to my self-improvement and goals. It felt fun and rejuvenating to pull out my work every day.

A lot of times when I was really busy, I would work from my bubble bath at the end of the day. I would prop my board up against the head of my pink oval tub and imagine experiencing all that was on my board. I took notes on my progress. I tried to read every book I was studying that would help me reach my goals carefully, dissecting the ideas one by one.

The one I lingered on a lot under the Love section was a little picture I drew of two stick people. They represented Rusty and me. I drew white sand and a big sun shining down as water lapped at our legs. That picture always made me sigh with contentment. I felt like I was looking at my future. I set aside my goal board and closed my eyes in bliss in the bathtub.

I started my journey of self-empowerment and personal improvement in 1977. Over ten years, I recorded my major improvements - I wrote:

MAJOR CHANGES IN MY LIFE - 1977 to 1987:
- ✓ *I am a happy family person.*
- ✓ *A good wife and a good mother.*
- ✓ *I stopped smoking.*
- ✓ *I stopped drinking.*
- ✓ *I am a good housekeeper.*
- ✓ *I look better than I ever have.*
- ✓ *I am kinder, more understanding, and giving.*

That's a damn good start, I thought. And it all started with me understanding that I was part of God. I say "God," but others may call this divine power by other names. These goals were no longer wants, but things I accomplished for myself by learning what I had to do to make these goals happen. My heart told me God was good. If I believed that to be true, then he couldn't make bad consequences happen in my life. Nothing could "just happen".

I had to achieve results with my brain, my learning tool that affects my mind. When I was younger, I held bad ideas about myself and believed them to be true. Now, knowing that I had free choice, I produced what I believed. Believing that I was no more than unwanted crabgrass was why I would feel depressed and angry. I behaved according to those thoughts. Now, I was deliberately filling my head with good ideas.

Was I a new, changed person? I didn't lead a vastly different life, not at first. The big difference was how I was teaching my mind to operate. It didn't matter how many times things went wrong and I messed up. I had my goal board. I kept my mind filled with what I wanted to see in my life. Now instead of reading romantic novels in my spare time, I was reading everything I could find about the power of the mind. I read ideas about how things worked as universal laws.

I was also learning how to pray more effectively. Yes, I believed in a higher power. That was the one thing every book and every religion seemed to have in common. This was a methodology that held me accountable for my receiving. I can pray to be a kinder human being, but if I still focused on the negative things about a person, whether it was true or not, how could more kindness and love flow into me?

I learned that I could acknowledge the negativity that exists in a person, but to change, I had to react to people differently. It required discipline to keep my brain from getting caught up in instant reactions. This was put to the test right when I was learning to discipline my mind.

We rented a house in Clermont, Florida for the winter in the 2000s. Rusty wanted to take his motorcycle so he could ride with his brother, who was living in Naples with his wife Darlene. The day after we arrived, our doorbell rang. Standing at the front door was a woman who didn't bother to introduce herself. She stood there with her arms crossed, fuming mad. She wasn't here to welcome us to the community.

"May I help you?" I asked her.

"Hi, yeah. I hit the trailer that you have backing out of my driveway. But it's not my fault. You have no right to park that thing here, and you need to fix this."

"Oh my. Wait just a minute, let me get my husband," I said.

Rusty and I walked out to look at the damage to the trailer, and it was significant. There was a large dent and scratches on the trailer. The woman's car was mostly OK, just a small scratch. But you'd have thought she was the injured party with her actions. The woman reminded us again that it wasn't her fault, that we had no right to park here.

"I'm done with this," the woman announced.

"Wait a minute, we need your insurance information," Rusty told her. He was getting a little mad. I put my hand on his arm to calm him down. Getting mad at her while she was already agitated was not going to do any good. I had to keep telling myself that too. I thought carefully.

"Please? It will only take a minute," I said.

"No, were done. I'm taking my kids to school." She got in her car and took off. Her kids in the back seat watched us through the window.

Of course, we couldn't leave things like this. Rusty and I called the police. The police officer said if the woman refused to give us her information, to call back. He would get it from her. He also told us we had every right to be parked in front of our house. We confronted the woman when she got home that evening. If anything, her attitude had gotten worse.

"I am not giving you anything, this is not my problem!" she yelled at us.

"Well, when the police were here today--" I said.

"What, you called the police on me? How dare you! I wasn't the one in the wrong," she said.

My heart jumped. This was one of those times that I could have felt justified in harboring all kinds of nasty words and thoughts about this situation and this woman. But that would not, in any way, benefit me by putting those hateful feelings in my body. I stood my ground. I looked her straight in the face and spoke with a very patient voice.

"Look, we had something important to us and you damaged it. Instead of ringing our bell and just saying you were sorry for the damage, you started attacking us. And if you had given us your information, we wouldn't have involved the police. We could have taken care of this, neighbor to neighbor."

The woman didn't take that well. With one last nasty sentence out of her mouth, she got in her car and drove away again. I didn't know what to say. We had no choice but to call the police again to get the insurance information.

A few weeks later I answered the door and the same woman was standing there. This time her posture was different, and her eyes were averted.

"I owe you an apology. You were right. I should never have behaved like that. I am a Christian woman, and I am so sorry. I was just so upset that day," she said.

I don't think anyone would have blamed me if I had treated her the way she had treated me. But I chose at that moment, to remember my desire to be a better, kinder, person. I couldn't be better if I reacted automatically without thinking first. I carefully organized what to say.

"I forgive you. Thank you for stopping by," I said.

The woman looked at me like she couldn't believe that I was being civil about this.

"I was wrong about you. You were nothing but patient the entire time. Thank you, thank you," the woman said.

I smiled at her, and asked if her car was okay. We spoke a little, but she didn't stay long. I felt happiness bloom inside of me. I don't know if I made a difference, but I would like to think that I helped. Maybe I changed her mind for the better out of that stressful situation. My inside world, my soul soup, was becoming better and better. I was reaching toward one of my goals to be a kinder person to myself and others. I couldn't wait to write this down in my diary.

Chapter 26

Some people hold the same beliefs I do. A few people get backed off by the idea that they have responsibility for receiving prayer. In other words, I believe that I can't just pray for positive change or an outcome that I want to happen. I can't just leave it up to divine power as if it's a wish fulfillment genie. I believe that I have a responsibility to take as many actions and steps as I can to see my prayer manifest in my life.

I often wondered how God worked at a football game. Both sides are praying to win. One side will lose. The same prayers are being said. Both sides have a goal to win that game. That is where I believe we come to the equation. Maybe one player on each side has the same desire and says the same prayer. One football player prayed, *"Please let my team win that game on Friday night,"* and turned it over for God to deliver the answer. Having said his prayer, the football player went on about his week.

But what if the opposing team member did the same thing? But instead of just bowing his head and saying his prayer, he kept his desire to win front and center. He thought about what he would need to do to help make the win possible. He practiced more on the field, whether or not it rained or shined. The opposing football player helped his team give it everything they had at practice. He was conscious that he had to do his part to make it happen, not just pray one time and hope God came through. The football player watched what he ate and drank. He got good rest each night. He rallied his team together. This player did his part in receiving his prayer. I know who I would put my money on to win the football game on Friday night.

For me, it's not the writing down or looking at pictures that brought my results. It's keeping the desire or prayer constantly active in my thoughts, so I could better respond to how or what my next step should be. Cutting out a picture of money in my hand doesn't put the money in my hand, but it does keep me excited and hopeful in the full belief that I can obtain my financial wealth goal on my goal board. Rusty and I always had a good income, but that alone does not equal financial security. We were spending as much, and at times even more, than what was coming in.

When I concentrated on the Wealth portion of my board, my main focus was understanding how to get from no real savings and not always getting the bills paid on time, to real Financial Security. I created my plan with a few steps:

Step 1. Establish better credit.

Step 2. Get a good job for myself with benefits.

Step 3. Have confidence in my ability to do a good job. Pay all my bills on time.

My other financial goal was to have necessary bills paid on time each month for gas, electricity, etc. I always wanted to have several thousand dollars in my checkbook for "just in case" situations that popped up. I also wanted to keep my home beautiful and well-maintained. I tried to get these things accomplished many, many times in the past, but for some reason could not make the desire stick long enough to get to real, lasting results. This time I knew I could do it.

The first thing I did was make a spreadsheet. I wanted to make a record of what was coming in and when money needed to go out. My spreadsheet showed me the whole month at a glance. The next thing we needed to do, was to stop relying on Rusty's overtime, which made a sizable difference over a standard forty-hour paycheck. Now, I used all our overtime money to pay off bills or put it in savings.

Of course, this practice allowed our credit scores to automatically go up. I had built up enough confidence by now that I felt ready to work for a big company. I started work at Champion Spark Plug Company in the International Sales Division in 1987. We were still living in Ohio. Some of our families were still living there also. Doing paperwork to get a product out of the country is not an easy job. But this job paid more than I had ever made. It also came with a 401k. Within ten years we had great credit, no bills, and plenty of extra money in checking. We had worked and made our modest home into a home that we could be proud of. I had my board, and notebooks full of my practices and ideas. Now I was living my dream.

Just when I thought I had figured out how my life worked--*Wham!*-- my faith was put to the test. Rusty had worked and lived in Hawaii right before he was going to retire. Rusty and I had spent a whole winter there. Bob was grown up and on his life path. Kona, Hawaii, is breathtaking. The water was a deep, crystal blue. It was always temperate, and there was often a cool breeze that blew through the trees. The housing in the area we lived in was a beautiful three-story condo, across the street from the ocean. It was a beautiful representation of how I envisioned Hawaii before I came to visit.

The only surprising thing about this area is seeing all that black lava. You have to look hard to find the big, white sandy beaches indicative of Hawaii. I had one sandy beach I went to. It was called "Disappearing Beach". Sometimes the sand was there and sometimes it wasn't, due to the tides and prevailing winds in the area. Rusty worked five days a week, so that left the evenings and weekends to explore. It was such a wonderful experience that we vowed to go back, but without him having to work.

Rusty had made lots of friends over in Hawaii. One day, he got a call from a guy named Scott. He had worked with Rusty a few times and he was friendly enough, although quite full of himself when I met him. Over the course of the conversation, Scott told Rusty he bought one of the condos that had been under construction the previous year. We instantly knew what complex he was talking about. Rusty told him what our plans were about coming over again for a vacation stay. Scott was a traveler that worked all over the country. He told us he was going to be back in Hawaii in a few weeks to buy some furniture for the condo.

These were beautiful condos that were across the street from the ocean. He offered it to us for the upcoming winter months. We couldn't believe our luck. We agreed on the payment, and he said he would get back to us when he was over there. He asked if there were any special things I needed in the kitchen for cooking.

Wow, this is like another dream coming true!

Scott's offer allowed us to have a wonderful opportunity. Rusty and I wanted to make it happen. We talked to Scott several times on the phone after we went back home to Ohio.

"Oh no, everything is fine over here," Scott said.

"That's great to hear. Do you need me to wire you a security deposit or the first month's rent upfront?" Rusty asked.

The both of us were in the kitchen. Rusty angled the phone towards me so I could listen in.

"Don't worry, I don't need any of that yet. I'd rather take care of a few things before I even get to that point. We have plenty of time to work that out," Scott said.

My eyebrows raised and I grinned at Rusty. He smiled back.

We booked our airline tickets. We wanted to share this vacation with our loved ones, so we offered trips of two-week stays, for Rusty's parents, my sister Donna and her husband, and my cousin Jack and Pat. Our son Bob was going to stay with us for a month, now that he was an adult. Everyone booked their tickets for their designated two-week stays. We were all so excited. We couldn't wait for Christmas to be over so we could get on a plane and fly away, to the beauty of Hawaii.

Scott was starting to give us more and more excuses about why he hadn't gotten back to Hawaii to furnish the place. We were getting close to the start of our trip. Time was running out for Scott to make good on his word. All along I had prayed over every aspect of this vacation. Rent that we could afford: Check. Air flights for the exact dates we wanted: Check. Flights cheap enough that everyone could afford them: Check. I checked off all the steps, one by one, as my prayers were fulfilled. But something was missing.

We were not getting many calls from Scott anymore. It was about a month before we were scheduled to fly out of Ohio. Rusty kept calling him until Scott had to answer. We were in the kitchen again. I stood off to the side, my arms crossed. I could hear every word over the phone.

"We just want to know what's happening, Scott," Rusty said.

There was a pause over the phone. "Well, the condo doesn't actually belong to *me*, it belongs to my girlfriend."

Rusty's jaw started to clench. He spoke calmly over the phone, but I wasn't listening anymore. There was white noise in my head. Heat filled my blood. I took a step back. *This can't be happening. Not less than a month before our trip. Not when everyone I invited was so excited about going to Hawaii.*

Rusty looked at me.

"Mary, Scott wants to talk to you," Rusty said.

I shook my head. I didn't trust my voice. I left the room and opened a sliding door to the backyard. The winter chill bit into my skin underneath my sweater. There was absolutely no way I could be civil right now. All of my plans and prayers crumbled in my head. We had done so much work to make this trip happen. I believed in it with all my heart. I had prayed. And now, it wasn't going to happen after all that work I put in? My lips trembled. I rubbed my arms under the gray sky.

"Why, God?" I whispered, over and over again.

How could anyone do something like this? Scott certainly wasn't trying to scam us out of money, because we didn't wire him a penny. Our families had trusted me, and now I had to let them down. This new exasperation was too heart-wrenching. My thoughts spiraled. My belief crumbled. At that moment I had lost all my faith, every bit of it. If what I believed was true about putting actions behind your prayers, how could I possibly be in this situation? I no longer believed in any kind of divine power.

I pulled myself together long enough to let everyone know what happened. Rusty's parents, Donna, Bob, and my cousins were all as shocked as I was. But like I told Rusty before I even made the first phone call, I was determined to make this trip to Hawaii happen, somehow. This time I wasn't going to rely on a divine power or prayer. This trip was going to happen out of my actions, not my faith.

With just a short time to go, Scott was still trying to convince us that everything was going to work out for us to rent the condo. This time he was calling us with promises. If I could have crawled through that phone, that man would have been hairless by the time I got done with him. I couldn't remember the last time I had been that mad. How could someone do something like this?

I stopped praying. I stopped my daily meditations. I was a non-believer. It was like I was the player on the football team that did everything right. I prayed, I watched what I ate, and I practiced until my muscles were burning with pain. But when the game happened on Friday night, I still lost. *God must not be real after all.*

That was how I felt. God wasn't real. Things just happen, with no rhyme or no reason at all.

All I was concerned with now was making this vacation happen for my family. I needed to find a new place for us to stay in Hawaii, and fast. The plane tickets were expensive, so we didn't want to lose our travel dates. But it wasn't just about the money we paid. I knew how crushed my family would be if they couldn't make the trip because of someone else's foolishness. We talked so much about all the things we would do and the places we wanted to see. And the best part for all of us was getting away from the cold, snow, and dark grey skies that seemed like a daily occurrence in Ohio that winter. I was going to make this vacation happen for myself and my family, one way or another.

I contacted the travel agency that found us a place to stay the previous year. I hounded them every day. You don't get a winter rental at the last minute in Kona, Hawaii. But I was determined. I was like a bulldog that wouldn't give up his chew toy. Finally, they found a place that I could rent for three months at a price that was much higher than what Scott was going to charge us, but it was doable. Financially, we could still do it. And schedule wise, everyone could go without having to change their tickets. I let out a sigh of relief after I got off the phone. *I did it.*

After all the problems and hard work, I couldn't wait to plop down on a lounge next to the pool in Hawaii and bask in the bright, warm sun.

As I relaxed, my mind drifted to the fact that I no longer believed in any kind of higher power. It wasn't about the actual trip that almost didn't happen. I realized that something was off deep inside me. I had lost my connection to an intrinsic part of myself. I felt empty. My spirituality was my everything. It defined who I was. I had spent decades learning and practicing these principles. It had been my lifeline, my whole life.

My spirituality was connected to the worst and best moments in my life. I always believed that my connection to the divine was also connected to the strength and protection my little girl gave me in my vulnerable years. But I walked away from all that. I walked away from that part of my heart. Each time, spirituality came knocking, I refused to answer the door. I was just here, living my everyday life. What happens, happens, end of story. I went on like that for several months. I ignored the emptiness inside.

A year later I was cleaning underneath the bed. My fingers bumped against paper and hard cover bindings. I brought out all my dusty writings and books that I kept since 1977. The covers were starting to peel. Some of the pages were turning yellow. The spines were worn in with cracked lines. I spread my books and work out, uncertain of how I felt. Do I throw these away, or do I keep them? So much of my life was contained in these papers. but if the process didn't work, what was the point in keeping them?

Chapter 27

I looked through them again. I couldn't put the books and my old writings down. It took me back to my early problems and all the things that had changed in my life. My writings detailed my thoughts and feelings. I exposed my heart about my father passing away, the changes from my mother, the hell I lived in with Tom, Donna's birth, moving to Kentucky without friends or family, giving birth in New Jersey, meeting Rusty, and so much more. I was amazed at how much I had changed from those years.

This was a good track record. I knew it wasn't just a coincidence that my life changed so drastically. Things didn't just happen in my life. I was saved when I needed help. I went down bitter paths in my thinking. I climbed out of old habits. I had grown so many times.

I don't know how long I read my writings. I set aside my cleaning for the day. I sat in my favorite chair by the window. Rusty was out. I took a deep breath and closed my eyes. I started to meditate for the first time in many, many months. I used colors most of the time to help focus when I meditated. I would imagine a single color in my mind. I would allow that color to flow into my body from head to toe. I would think about how that color makes me feel, and what it means to me emotionally and visually. I sat still and kept my eyes closed. The first color that came to mind was red.

A rich hue flooded my mind. I could see a coffee mug in my kitchen, and the rose petals in my neighbor's garden. Red was the color of passion, whether good or bad. I allowed the color red to fill my mind and flood my body like heat. I allowed myself to feel love and anger in equal measure. These were the feelings that came to mind. I took a steady breath. I let it all go—the color, my feelings, and the visual connections.

I imagined the next color. Red bled into orange hues. Orange brightened into sunshine yellow. I thought of Bob's nursery when he was just a baby. I moved on to the next color. Yellow blended into a rich green. The color of grass, weeds, and the stem of a daisy. Green deepened into shades of blue, then violet. I stood up. My meditation didn't end. I left my bedroom, still focused on the color violet. The color of night becoming darker in the sky.

The shadows in the hallway took on a sharper feeling. I stood in front of a window and closed my eyes. I let the warmth of the sun soothe me. The violet color in my mind brightened until it reached a lilac shade. The hue blended like the dawn, the coming of another day after a night of shaking and darkness. I opened my eyes to the sun. *White.* I reached the color white in my mind. I felt an energy surge through me. Brightness filled my being. *I am awake, I am whole, and I am ready.*

I felt the same energy that had held my hand when I was a little girl. This divine power was holding my hand now that I was all grown up. I couldn't feel it these last few months because I stopped believing. But divine power had not left me; it was there the whole time. Now, this same divine let me know I had gotten EXACTLY what I had wanted. I wanted to spend a whole winter in Hawaii, without Rusty having to work. I received that. I wanted to share this adventure with our families, and I received that.

Our families made memories we would treasure our whole lives. We circled the whole island. We visited a volcano. I walked on black lava. I felt the heat coming through the ground under the brightness of the sun. I was able to lounge with Donna. I laughed joyfully with my son as he bought his fiancée's engagement ring. I walked along the beach with Rusty, hand in hand.

So, what had gone wrong? There were stumbling blocks I had to overcome to make this vacation happen. My belief that this divine power should be simple and perfect was an unequivocal yes and yes. When I had so many problems to overcome, it felt like I was on the wrong road. I figured this power did not work the way I thought it should. So, therefore it didn't exist. I could just as easily think, *"All these problems have been put in my way, so I will accept this as the will of God and stop trying."*

But after that meditation, it was laughable to me how my brain's thoughts had taken me so off course. Pre-programmed emotions had taken over because Scott offended me. Frustration and anger had been my downfall. Those little devils could just sneak into your brain so easily when you're upset because of someone else's actions. But now I understood.

The lesson I learned here was twofold. First, I learned that with enough roadblocks to overcome, how very "easy" it is to stop believing. Years of research on religions and dozens and dozens of books read on the power of the mind, seminars, and years of proven results, and *Poof!* I stopped believing that easily. It was embarrassing to realize I did that. It humbled me. The second part of this learning experience was the realization that we never stop evolving.

Yes, I stopped believing in divine power to be there for me. But when I returned to this part of myself, I had more knowledge to work with. With each set back I gained knowledge and understanding about how I was connected to my physical body, my thought processes, and how my spiritual body can be connected to all things. The need for understanding never stops, no matter how much my life changed or how old I got.

As the saying goes, "one thing leads to another". Since I began my search for self-improvement in 1977 through seminars, books, self-reflection, and personal writings, here I was again searching for more knowledge through books, classes, and notes. I'd been learning and practicing for several decades. Now it was time to get back into a new level of learning.

"The Power of Your Sub-Conscious Mind" by Joseph Murphy was a powerful book. This man was born in 1898 and wrote this book in 1963. In 2011 they were still reprinting the book. I read a book about a system of higher logic of the infinite, or the third canon of thought as discussed in *A Key to the Enigmas of the World* by P.D. Ouspensky. There are some things I couldn't wrap my mind around because I didn't have the foundation to understand. Ouspensky, Einstein, Hawking, and lots of others believe that time and space are the same. All these years later, I am just beginning to grasp how that could be.

So now, thinking back to that Hawaii setback that took me so off course that year, but brought me to more understanding, I realize it was up to me. It was my choice. I could have stopped believing and never returned to my spirituality. We are always free to choose what we believe in. More knowledge brings more questions. And for me, that describes the purpose of life. Gathering collective knowledge. It's the road we all must travel. Just because I can't fully grasp higher dimensions as some can, doesn't mean they don't exist.

I reflected on my little board full of pictures and actualized my life. My goal board was a tiny baby step to a better life. I was continuing to soak in knowledge learned from those that went down the road before me. We can learn bad things as well as good things from the experiences we have in life. I learned to think negatively about my father's passing, which affected my self-worth for years until I unlearned that damaging perception.

My parents had a negative view of welfare. I didn't understand why as a child. Maybe it was something learned from society or other people that wasn't always true. Maybe if my parents had taken baby steps to unlearn their perception about welfare, my experiences, and the experiences my siblings went through would have been different. I believe that we are capable of learning great good, just as much as we are capable of learning terrible perceptions.

I learned a great lesson going to Disney World one year when Bob was still a child in the 1970s. It was a sunny, cloudless day in Orlando, Florida. Small families navigated the new park with balloons in hand and licking ice cream cones from the stands. Some buildings were not complete yet. When we walked up to Cinderella's Castle a guy was working on the small tiles going up through the center of the castle. This job was massive. I had to ask him.

"Sir, I'm curious. How are you going to get all of this done?"

He said something I will never forget. The man pointed to a section that he completed.

"This is what I can realistically do in one day. I know that, so when I come to work, I'm only interested in making sure I get that much done. I don't think about getting the whole thing done. I only concentrate on the now."

He was doing his baby steps just like I was doing my baby steps. The world got much easier to maneuver after I realized the truth of that statement.

Chapter 28

With my faith firmly in place again I took stock of the balance of my life. I felt content. That was a feeling that eluded me for a great portion of my life growing up and for a lot of my adult life. I realized that the main ingredients in my soul soup were building a harmonious flavor, better than anything I ever had before. Health and Wealth were the main ingredients to my soul soup, along with Love and My Expressions. Together they created a strong, aromatic, and healthy flavor that I always wanted to taste. Everything was working in harmony. I couldn't get enough of the contentment I felt.

The world was no longer something I had to protect myself from. My inner little girl had grown up with me at last. She no longer had to guard my mind and keep everything good and bad hidden behind a closed door. I didn't have to rely on a system I built up to protect myself. I was more involved with the present, and more whole than at the beginning of my story. Life was good. Everything seemed to flow smoothly. I felt like I had climbed a mountain. I was standing at the top with my arms outstretched, yelling, *"I did it! I did it!"*

Only to have a roaring wind come along. I rolled halfway down the mountain before I could stop, my heart in my throat, arms shaking off the edge.

The windstorm was the death of Rusty's mother. Her death was not a shock, but my reaction to it was. She'd been fighting bone cancer for a long time. They moved her from the hospital into a hospice center. Each day she slipped a little closer to the other side. I was close to my mother-in-law. Our homes were within walking distance for many years. She was the "grandma on the side" to us. Rusty's mother was there for me when I needed a caretaker for Bob when I was a new mother, struggling with my husband's frequent outings. She helped build the beautiful nursery in sky blue and sunshine yellow colors. She was the first one to ask me to call her "Mom" when my heart was still fragile from the jagged relationship with my mother.

Rusty's mom had taken me under her wing and taught me many things I needed to learn. At one point I had thought of her as the mom I had always wanted. As the years passed, she became a much different person, as did I. We were not as close as we once were. But none of that could explain the fear that was shooting through my body every time I went to the hospital, especially when she was put into hospice care. It felt like death was all around me.

I tried to keep it all in. Rusty and Bob needed me now. Our son was grown, married, and living on his own in Ohio, but his heart was hurting too. I had to keep it together for them. I did a good job for a few days. But one night I couldn't sleep. I couldn't keep my eyes shut. I couldn't move, even though I was wide awake. *Not again, please.*

The sun came up. The light poured through my bedroom window. I was able to stand, but my whole body had uncontrollable shaking. I recognized these symptoms. This happened to me before. When I was afraid to be a new mother when Bob was just a baby, I went through this horrible event. I was shocked. *How could this happen again?* I took steady breaths. *I have to keep moving*, I thought.

I carefully made my way downstairs. I was still shaking. Rusty took one look at me in the kitchen and rushed to my side.

"Mary, what in God's name is going on? You're shaking all over, are you all right?" Rusty asked.

He put his arms around me to try and stop the shaking. We had been sleeping in separate bedrooms because of his snoring, so this was the first he had seen me since the night before.

"I'll be fine. I just need to get to the doctor's and see Jeff," I said.

Jeff Lewis had been our family physician for a couple of decades. He always made good recommendations for specialist treatment. He had come to my rescue when I found myself in Tarpon Springs, Florida, with a broken neck and couldn't move. In Tarpon Springs, I fell in the bathroom. I was unable to move for over two hours until Rusty came home and found me. I was seen at the hospital, but the doctors couldn't find any swelling or protrusions wrong with my neck. The X-rays didn't show anything wrong either and nothing was visible on my neck except for extreme swelling. However, I knew something was wrong because I couldn't move. I wanted better care from my primary doctor.

We couldn't get back home for a month. I was bedridden and in a neck brace, sipping water from a dropper and eating carefully from my bed. It was terrible. But I knew that if I could get through this, I could get through anything. We were able to drive home and see Dr. Lewis. He saw the X-rays taken at the hospital in Tarpon Springs. He immediately made an appointment with a neurosurgeon who took new X-rays. He found something amazing. The third vertebrae in my neck had fused perfectly back in place. I did not have paralysis or any other life-altering issues. The only thing I had to do was wear a neck brace for six months.

The neurosurgeon told me at the time, "Mary, if your vertebrae hadn't fused this well I would have had to put you in a halo."

He declared my recovery a complete miracle. My neck had healed over time with careful support on its own when the hospital in Tarpon Springs hadn't found anything wrong at first.

So I knew that if I could just get to Jeff's office with my uncontrollable shaking, I would be fine. But right now, my focus was on getting Rusty out the door and to his mother's side without me. I spoke in a calm voice.

"I'll call Donna. She can stay with me until I can get an appointment to see Jeff."

Rusty's lips pressed into a tight line. "I don't like this. I'm staying right here."

I let out a shaky breath. "Mom needs you, Rusty."

He shook his head and guided me into a seat at the table. Rusty ran into the living room to get a pillow to put behind my back.

"You need me right now, Mary."

"But we don't know how much time Mom has left with us. I could never forgive myself if something happened just because of me-- because of *this*."

I begged him with my eyes. Rusty watched me, torn over what to do. After much convincing, he left.

My sister Donna and her husband Carl arrived a little later. They were in shock when they saw me at the kitchen table. Rusty had left the door unlocked for them. Donna gasped when she saw me. I couldn't go upstairs and get properly dressed. I was still in my night clothes, my hair was still undone from a restless night before.

"Mary, you're scaring the shit out of me," Donna whispered. She took my shaking arms into her hands. "What's going on?"

"I think I'm having a panic attack," I whispered. No one had ever told me about this. I wasn't diagnosed with panic attacks. I learned the words "panic attack" through my self-study.

"Why, what happened?" Donna asked.

"I can't think about anything but her dying, and I don't know why," I trembled.

Donna sucked in a breath. "I think you need to go to the hospital if you've been like this all night."

"No, I'm going to put a call into Jeff as soon as the office opens."

Donna frowned. "Are you sure he'll be able to fit you in today? Because I think you have to see someone as soon as possible."

"I have to try," I said.

Jeff was booked solid, but he got me an appointment with another doctor for that morning. Donna buckled me in. She closed the door and jumped in the front passenger seat with Carl at the wheel. When I arrived, I was still shaking. As I walked into the room, the nurse asked me if I was shaking because I was cold.

I started to cry. "No."

The nurse took my vitals. My blood pressure was extremely high. She kept asking questions before the doctor arrived. All I could do was say, "I don't know, I don't know."

I don't remember Donna or Carl being in the exam room with me. I could hardly recall how I got to this point. The room was bright. Medical tools were everywhere, along with posters on the walls. I wasn't paying much attention. I tried to hang on to the exam table, to focus on breathing through my tears and fear dripping in my brain. The nurse looked at me with concern.

"Ma'am, are you physically hurting anywhere?" she asked.

"My chest hurts," I whispered.

My shaking hand slowly rubbed a spot over my heart. The nurse went and got a machine. She attached wires all over my chest. She was with me for a long time, focused on her work. I finally started to calm down enough to tell her what was happening. A sweet, female doctor stepped into the room. She took my hand and introduced herself as Dr. May. She had a soft voice and a gentle smile. I didn't know how much I needed that. I gave her my name when she asked.

"The good news is that your heart is fine, but you are obviously under severe stress. Do you think you can tell me why?"

"My mother-in-law is dying, and I can't stop thinking about it. We used to be so close. She'd done so much for me, and now she's just leaving--just like that, and there's nothing I can do. I have so much to do. My husband and my son need me, but I can't stop shaking," I said.

Dr. May nodded. "Mary, under these circumstances I would normally admit you, but I do understand your need to be there for your family. I have some medication that I can prescribe for now, to help get you through the funeral. But I'm going to schedule you to come back next week and see Dr. Lewis. I've already spoken to him, and he feels like you'll be ok. And if you're not, you are to call him right away."

I was okay with that. I just needed something for now, just to get me through this. I needed to be there for my family, in the here and now. Not trapped in my fearful mind.

The next day, I awoke calm and clear-headed. I felt dread that the shakes could return. I was prescribed one Ativan 0.5, three times a day. I could tell I wasn't out of the woods yet. I could feel anxiety set in when it would be time for me to take the next pill. They did keep me calm, and I handled everything that I needed to do. Everyone knew what had happened to me. But I handled the preparations for the memorial, and for caring for others' broken hearts.

Chapter 29

The next week I went in to see Dr. Lewis at the WW Knight Family practice. This place was also a teaching facility for interns. When I was shown in the exam room, an intern first talked to me. I don't know if it was because I didn't know him, or because I had been strained to the maximum, but I started to cry. The intern looked at me surprised.

"Ma'am, what's wrong?" he asked.

"I think I know why I had those panic attacks," I managed to say. "My father's suicide…Everything goes back to that."

Gut-wrenching sobs came out of me. The intern urged me to stay right where I was. He dashed out of the room. When Jeff came in, I could barely talk.

"Mary, hold on, I will be right back," Dr. Lewis said.

He came back with a therapist that was on staff at the practice. A woman with a calm manner walked into the room. I swiped under my eyes and looked up at her.

"Mary, my name is Nancy Delaney. Do you mind if I ask you some questions?"

I swallowed. "Okay."

Nancy asked me some general questions. I started to calm down. She spoke to me as if I were a friend and not a patient that needed to be clinically analyzed. Her voice and behavior had a very positive effect on me. We talked for quite a while. She asked me if I would schedule an appointment to see her the next day. The doctor left, and she stayed behind. I immediately agreed. Nancy's kind and intelligent eyes searched my face.

"Mary, you're not going to keep that appointment tomorrow, are you?" Nancy asked.

My eyes widened in surprise. "No, I promise I'll be back."

She nodded. "Okay then, I'll see you tomorrow."

I didn't have to convince myself that I needed help. This whole thing came from out of the blue, at least that's what it felt like. I thought I had reached the mountaintop in my life. I had worked on my goal board. I made strides in dealing with my trauma and issues through self-study. I felt contentment. But this panic attack at the loss of Rusty's mother was a wake-up call. The work I'd begun was not finished. It was time for me to seek outside help.

Sometimes I can see and feel someone's true nature in their eyes and their manner. I immediately felt safe with her. If Jeff thought she could help me, I knew she could. He was the one who recommended an appointment with her. I would do my best to work through everything I couldn't see about myself on my own.

It wasn't immediate, but as months passed, I opened up more and more in my appointments with Nancy. Unlike the psychiatrist I first saw many years ago after my first panic attack, Nancy Delaney's office was more like visiting someone's home. It was small and comfortable. There was a small sofa. A little bookcase was pushed against a wall. The colors in the room were calming and soft. Her office didn't smell sterile or look like a traditional doctor's office. I felt relaxed when I sat on her couch.

Nancy started with easy and gentle questions. She already went over my medical file. She remembered the reason for my first visit when she met me. The two of us started with baby steps.

"Have you ever done therapy before, Mary?"

"No. I saw a psychiatrist after my son Bob's birth many years ago, but he didn't help me."

"Have you ever experienced a panic attack like that before?" she asked.

"Yes, but I wasn't prescribed any medication. The term 'Panic Attack' was never used. I guess with everything else I had experienced, the psychiatrist probably assumed I knew the term, but back then things like this were not talked about. At all."

I didn't know it existed. Maybe Ativan 0.5 wasn't invented yet. I wasn't sure. I remembered how back then, everyone thought I was just going to the hospital to get attention when I felt like I couldn't breathe, and my blood pressure was sky high. But the fear in my heart and mind was real. It wasn't something that I could just turn on or off.

"Would you like to tell me how you coped before coming here?" Nancy gently asked.

I swallowed. We were going to get closer to the thoughts and feelings in my heart. I gave her general answers at first. I wasn't afraid to tell her some of the horrible mistakes I had made. For some reason that was what I was focused on. *I was a horrible person!*

In our conversations, it felt like old, pre-programmed thoughts were coming back. But I knew that this time, instead of writing it down or meditating on it, I was getting it off my chest for the first time. I never shared the darker parts of my heart with anyone else, not even my loved ones.

"I hadn't been a good mother or wife. I was selfish and self-centered. I didn't care about others. Even though everyone thought I was a nice person, I knew that wasn't true." I said.

I thought I'd made peace with those thoughts. Why was this happening now? Over the weeks and months, Nancy addressed each thing I had said about myself. She unstrung them, one by one. She helped me see why I did the things I did. Why my choices were natural considering the events that happened to me, that molded me into who I was. I was no different from anyone else. I just had a set of different problems to face.

Nancy helped me understand that I had forgiven myself on the surface. True change is felt, not known. She taught me how to stay in the present moment. I could use a simple exercise. Nancy pulled out a rubber band and gave it to me.

"I want you to try and wear this as much as possible. Slip it onto your wrist."

I took the brown rubber band and pushed it back until it was comfortably settled on my forearm. "Okay, but why?"

Was the rubber band supposed to help me remember something? Nancy smiled encouragingly.

"Anytime you feel the slightest inkling that you are disconnecting from reality because of something someone said or did, or if something unpleasant happens at the moment, snap the rubber band."

My eyebrows raised. It was certainly worth a shot. I discovered it helped once I learned to utilize the exercise. When Rusty and I had to go through his mother's things after she was laid to rest, I could feel the fear dripping into me, out of the painfulness of what we had to do. I pulled back the rubber band on my arm. I let it go. The quick snap and sharp sound jolted me back to the present moment. I took a deep breath. *I can do this*, I thought.

I could stay present, stay here where I was needed. And I did.

I was learning how to experience everything in the now. It would be the difference between thinking about a loved one, compared to being with them in person. It was a whole different experience. I realized that I had experienced forgiveness of myself with my mind, but not with my soul. Any setback I experienced made me wonder why things couldn't remain on the same trajectory. Why did something always seem to interfere, just when I thought I had things figured out? But I realized it was almost like a pattern. Things would go along perfectly until--*Bam!*-- another Hawaii-like event would leave me questioning, *"What is going on here?!"*

I would end up questioning whether the knowledge I was working with no longer worked for the present situation. I would end up trying to seek new knowledge when I became frustrated with what I thought I knew didn't work. But things always change. Change was a part of life.

I realize that I have my spot firmly set in this world. It is going slow enough now that I am comfortable and peaceful. But I can't get enough answers to my connection to the higher, divine power. I had read enough by this time to realize that it wasn't even a question of "if" a divine power exists, but to what degree was I able to understand it.

I say divine power, but that's because in my heart of hearts, I can't make myself believe that one religion is right and all the rest are wrong. Salvation for just one set, and oblivion for the rest? We have so very many religions in this world. One of my "digital staff helpers", named Google Chrome, listed over 4,300 religions in the current, modern world. Christianity, Islam, Judaism, Buddhism, Sikhism, Juche, and Zoroastrianism exist, just to name a few. To quote Steven Hawking, *"I believe the universe is governed by the laws of science. The laws may have been decreed by God, but God does not intervene to break the laws."*

Although this man considered himself an Atheist, this too strikes me as a belief in a higher power. Maybe it doesn't matter at all if we think of the higher power as God or Mohammad or Brahman or the No Boundary Proposal concept that some physicists believe. So what does all of this have to do with a little girl that couldn't face the world that she lived in? My therapist Nancy helped me reach true, heartfelt soul change through therapy. This was the evolution of my soul.

I grew up believing in God. I thought of him as a person up above the sky. An entity that would take care of me, and help me, when I was in need. That was the way I experienced divine power from the first time I said my prayers as a child. But I learned that life moves to a universal law of rhythm. Our lives can easily swing from one direction to its polar opposite, from times of good to times of bad. What mattered the most were my choices in these changes.

My actual choices, thoughts, and words created something for or against me. I had a say in my life. With spiritual knowledge, self-improvement shown in my results, and outside help, I walked a long distance on that path.

In the Hawaii incident, I plunged into an inferno of non-belief. Nothing good or permanent was gained from that, but the experience allowed me to gain more insight into how fragile my surface-level belief was. New knowledge is always available to a student looking. I learned how to get from where I was, to where I wanted to go, with the help of my spirituality. We are a fine team. Now I know to expect the Law of Change to happen in life. This is another universal law that says that nothing stays the same in life, and it's true. If life didn't change, I would never have accessed door after door, to a closer place where the real me resides. The real me is who I am in the here and now, mentally, emotionally, spiritually, and physically.

Years ago, I couldn't have understood the universal laws that I have uncovered. They have always been there. I just didn't know about them, so my life was harder to understand. Why things were the way they were, why they happened, and my personal choice in all of it. I didn't become aware until I had a real need for each piece of new knowledge as practical application to my life. They would have been just words on a paper that I couldn't have related to.

Chapter 30

By the time I was 30, all my aunts and uncles had passed away. Cancer and heart attacks took most of their precious lives. But my mom was still going strong. Mom and Donna had lived with us on and off for a few years after Tom left our lives forever. She also took a turn living at Ed's house. But we all know where she really wanted to be, which was with Dave.

When Mom was about 60, Dave asked her to permanently live with him. This was fine with all of us. She was happy and content in Rensselaer, Indiana, with Dave. And the best part was that Dave loved having her with him. But Mom still loved returning to New Jersey for family visits. She would call us several times a week to keep us updated on whatever new adventure cousin Jack had her on.

This was Jack Foster, one of Aunt Theresa's sons. He loved our mother. Just being around Jack was a party. He was a happy, funny, and caring guy. That was the way he always treated us. No wonder we loved him so much.

"Mary, I had a wonderful birthday party!" Mom said to me over the phone. Mom's birthday was June 6th. She turned 65 at the time. All of us kids were working. We couldn't make the trip to her party in New Jersey.

"Honey, I wish you could have been here," Mom said, in between sips of her morning coffee. I could almost see her fuzzy purple slippers swinging as she talked, sitting in a chair that was just a touch bigger than she was.

"I wish I could have been there too, Mom," I smiled.

"Are you sitting down? Because this news will knock you off your feet!" Mom cackled and coughed at the same time.

"Jack found Alice Cyr and she came to my party! You remember Alice, don't you, honey? She lived across the hall from us when we lived in the Westfield Acres."

"Of course I remember her, Mom, wow! But how in the world did Jack track her down?"

We lost track of the Cyr's family when we moved out of the Westfield Acres all those years ago. Alice was the girl that loved to gab with Mom and me over Pepsis. That was so long ago, when I was first getting into makeup and hairstyles.

Mom chuckled. "I guess a friend of a friend knew her and got her telephone number for Jack. I couldn't believe it when I saw her. Mary, we sat and talked for hours! She wasn't with Jimmy anymore, but she was doing okay for herself. She said she would stop by to see me again before I go home."

I could hear the smile in her voice, and I knew she was looking forward to it. Unfortunately, Mom didn't get to see Alice again. Not long after her birthday, Mom passed away. She had a massive heart attack. The rescue team got her heart started, but she didn't regain consciousness.

All five of us kids were living in different states. Dave's family lived in Indiana. Donna and Carl's family lived in Michigan, as did Ed and his family. Rusty and I lived in Ohio. Mom had become a big part of our lives after Tom left. We enjoyed being together. Forgiveness had worked in our lives. We couldn't bear to lose her now. Within a few days, we all made our way to New Jersey. Jack was with us, and so was

Rusty. A female doctor was waiting for us when we walked into the hospital.

"Your mother as you knew her is gone. These tubes are the only thing keeping her alive now."

It felt like the air was sucked out of the room. Disbelief showed on our faces.

"The rescue workers treated your mother for a long time, but they didn't do her any favors."

"But she might keep on living with the tubes in, right?" Donna asked.

The doctor glanced at her file. "This equipment could keep her going one more day, or one more year, or perhaps indefinitely. There's no way to be certain. This is a choice you all will have to make."

We could either leave the plugs in or disconnect her and hope for the best. I couldn't do it. Not yet. I ran out of the room and locked myself in the bathroom. My mind did not want to accept this new information. I could feel the shaking start. I fell to the floor. Wracking sobs escaped my heart. I heard Jack pounding on the door. I didn't want to, but I opened the door. I fell into his arms.

I knew I needed to be there. We needed to make a family decision, and the sooner the better. Each one of us was crushed. Sorrow, fear, and guilt ran through us. We handled it in our own way. But we would make this choice together. Whatever we did, we would do it as one family.

Dave had always been the closest to Mom. But we didn't mind. Dave has a faith that's so strong that I believe he could move a mountain. As hard as this was for him, he would meet this challenge knowing God would move all of us to the right decision. That was how his faith worked.

Ed had always been stoic. He would do whatever was needed to be done. He would be abrasive now, as he always had been. Ed is very quiet, taking all the information in before he makes a decision he could live with.

My sister Donna is an angel, although my brother Dave would not agree with that description. It is so much fun to watch them together. Donna had the heart to give to others. She has always been there for all of us. I believe her heart is filled with angel dust. When she leaves this world, her wings will be set back on her shoulders.

Now was the time that all of us, with our different personalities, had to sit down and decide our mother's fate. We made the unanimous decision to remove the breathing tube but to leave the feeding tube in place. Every one of us knew Mom would not want to exist as she was. Hell, we wouldn't want that for ourselves either. The feeding tube was in place, so if there was so much as a spark of life in her, then we had not decided her fate for her. She would decide what needed to be done for herself.

We waited several more days after the plug had been removed. There was no change to Mom's condition. We had been gone from our homes for over a week. We all had jobs to return to. Things that had to be taken care of. But we hated to leave.

Our Foster and Watson families were with us every day at the hospital. They brought us food. They stayed with Mom. They made us laugh when they could. It was because of all of them that we were able to leave knowing that our mother would be taken care of, just as if it was happening to their own mom.

We got home and all we could do was fall into bed. The very next morning, the phone rang. We were told that Mom had passed away. We felt like zombies getting clean clothes back into our suitcases. Jack met us at his door, his arms outstretched.

All of us went to the cemetery where our father had been buried in New Jersey. A captivating, beautiful woman greeted us. Rusty spoke for all of us.

"We're here to see if we can purchase a spot next to their father. This is where their mother wanted to be buried," my hero of a husband said.

The woman nodded. "Give me the name and I'll check the records for you."

She walked into another room and came back with a file. "It says here that a deposit was put down on the adjoining plot back in 1959 when your father was buried."

"What?" I blurted.

"Nothing else was ever paid on it?" Rusty asked.

"No, nothing," the woman said.

Rusty looked over the paperwork from 30-something years ago. "We would like to pay that balance, please."

"To be honest with you, I'm not sure we can sell that plot at all. The file mentions that the parcel is too small to sell. Let me get the cemetery sexton."

We waited for him to arrive. And who should walk in but the guy that Rusty had talked to for several days? This was when we'd been at the hospital together, waiting for news about Mom. Rusty's brows rose. The other man smiled at him.

"Wow, what a coincidence," Rusty told the cemetery sexton as they shook hands.

They spent a moment catching up about the families. The guy took the paperwork and started reading.

"Come on, let's go take a look at this spot," he said.

We walked over to where daddy was buried. The cemetery was immaculate. This hospital buddy of Rusty's looked over the spot where we wanted to bury Mom. He acknowledged that the plot was quite small. As he closed the file, he looked at us.

"We can make this work."

Our mom would get her wish to be buried next to my father. This wasn't just another case of a coincidence to me. It was a divine promise, given to us.

Epilogue

Decades and decades have passed, and my long-term goal board is still with me. All those years ago when I wrote them on that white box top, they had just been dreams. All those dreams are now a reality. In my Health section I wrote, *"I am healthy, calm, and peaceful. I still have plenty of energy. I know what it feels like to be full of Spiritual Grace, even though this comes and goes."* I also wrote under my Health section, *"I am accepting of myself; the older I get, the better I look for my age."*

I had a hard time reconciling those two thoughts. I was in my twenties when I wrote that. I had to accept that there is no way to stop aging from happening. Do nothing or do everything and it will still happen. Like everything else, I knew back then that just asking God to keep me looking good and healthy had no meaning, unless I figured out what I had to do. I realized it would take exercise and good eating for the rest of my life to accomplish that goal. Of course, I had help from a few good doctors along the way. I did my part, and the divine did the rest.

I am now seventy-three years old. For my birthday, I wore the dress that I bought to wear on my thirtieth birthday. It's a tight, form-fitting dress that made me feel wonderful that night. The dress is a sand-brown color. It's short-sleeved and long enough to just touch my calves, with an open back. I loved the way I looked in that dress. The first time Rusty saw me wearing it, he looked at me with wonder. I made a goal that night that when I was sixty, I would still look good wearing that dress. Every year from my thirtieth birthday to my seventy-third birthday I've put on that dress with a pair of heels. It hasn't failed me yet. Who knows, maybe I can make it to eighty in this dress. I think a healthy sex life keeps you young. My sensational, loving husband of fifty-five years thinks so too. Everything in my Health section has become a reality.

As far as my Wealth goals go, we are not extraordinarily wealthy, but I do have what I wanted all those years ago, which is financial security. We can pay cash for almost anything we would want. We can travel to any place we want. As I sit here writing these final pages, I do so from our retirement home in Florida. The fountains trickle with water into an aqua-colored pool. A pretty lake sits just yards beyond the pool. The beach, which calls to me often, is a short drive away. My little stick figure drawing of Rusty and me at the beach with water lapping at our legs and the sun shining brightly over us can now be a daily occurrence if we so choose. We both feel very blessed.

Under my Love goals, my exact wording was, *"To give love, and to feel loved"*. This portion of the goal board brought me the greatest change. I am extremely grateful for my results. I went from a little lost girl that sometimes could feel nothing because she'd been so damaged, to a confident woman that is not afraid to put herself out there and let the whole world see her flaws--and still be okay with her real self.

When Rusty and I renewed our vows on our fiftieth anniversary, the captain, photographer, and many passengers onboard the cruise ship told us we just radiated love. We cannot contain the love we feel for each other. For us this is pure, true love, which came from a lifetime of wanting to make the relationship work. The reward for all that work is living a daily life filled with joy and appreciation for each other. Were the old couple that you always see holding hands walking through stores and down the street of our neighborhood.

I don't act or react so far toward negative reactions, thoughts, and responses to life. I can flow so much better with the tides and changes. I started out wanting peace of mind for myself. For the most part, I have that. Some days I dwell in the feeling of my connection to divine power. In the Personal Self-Expression section of my goal board, I wrote: *"Realization of God through Constant Presence"*. In 2002 I added a note, *"I feel this is the most important"*.

How right I was. Things I couldn't comprehend in the past are made clearer, as more knowledge is absorbed. It's more than just knowing something that I have read, written, or studied. But it is about practicing, feeling, and being present. I learned that I should not hide or let myself become distant and automatic in life. This quest of mine will never end.

I know my life will contain problems to overcome. Change is a natural phenomenon. How our consciousness chooses to handle change, is what makes the difference. We are responsible for that. Dreams can be made real. They are our blueprints, and we are allowed to write them. This has been my truth, nothing more. I conquered many demons over the years, and I could not have done that without belief. Belief is malleable and needed for change.

We live together in this material world. The natural laws that pertain to the cosmos pertain to us also. Each person on this planet is different. Everyone's perception is different because of the way someone experiences life. When I first learned of my connection, I thought I could do anything. I would have times where I would struggle and times where I would succeed.

We're all on this journey together and when our soul guides us to new awareness and we share our experiences, we are all the better for it.

Am I a teacher? No.

Am I a philosopher? No.

Am I an expert on the universal laws presented here? No.

What I am is a survivor. And the most important thing I learned— the key ingredient to my soul soup: **DESIRE!**

I have a deep down, gut-wrenching desire not to accept the bad in my life. I couldn't accept it. I didn't accept it. And I will never accept it. I was knocked out of my safe, happy, loving world when I was ten years old. I fought back. I got knocked down. I fought. I got back up. Every time I got back up, I was one baby step closer to my goals.

The power to change resides in all of us, but it is a choice. Whether we deliberately choose to acknowledge it and use our brain as a learning tool is up to each one of us. I learned how to do it and I learned how to thrive, just one step at a time.

It worked.

Acknowledgments

I would also like to dedicate this book to my phenomenal husband Rusty. We did it! We never gave up on each other and here we are in love, 55 years later and still counting. We're reaping our rewards like two teenagers. I love you with every atom of my existence.

To Big Bad Bob: I love you too. You have always been my motivation and inspiration. And you still keep me laughing, my handsome son. I am very proud of you.

To my siblings: Telling me that my story "touched your soul and changed your life"—what wonderful words for a sister to hear. I love you. Always have, always will.

To Nancy Delaney, my trusted therapist: your skill and caring created the perfect environment that allowed me to transform from a weed into an orchid. Oh yes, thank you for telling me to write my book. :)

An immense thank you to my editor Jenel Northington. She knew what I wanted and patiently took me through the process, step by step. She really knows her business. I could not have gotten this book to print without her help.

To all my family and friends, if I talked about all of you individually this dedication would be as long as the book. So let me do this: **YOU, YES YOU!**

The ones that put a smile on my face and shared good memories with.

The ones that gave me a belly ache from laughing so hard.

The ones that confided in me and the ones I could confide in.

The ones I could always count on.

The ones that love me.

I thank you and appreciate you, and most of all, I love you. Thank you for all your inspiration.

About the Author

Mary is currently living in Florida with the love of her life and husband, Rusty Bilger. They've been married for 55 years and counting. She is still very close to her family, although they are scattered all over the country. Nothing makes her happier than a family reunion. The reason Mary wrote this book was to share her years of unrelenting search to overcome mental health issues, problems in her marriage, past trauma, and not having a drop of self-worth. She found her answers, and so can you.

Mary's Book List

Mary spent over 40 years learning how to become a better person. Her first step to self-awareness started by attending the world-renowned seminars of the brilliant Thomas D. Willhite, co-founder of PSI. What she learned then and still practices almost daily is that anything is possible if you don't give up. Her study took her to the old masters such as Robert Collier, Franklin Farrington, and P.D. Ouspensky. The following are suggested informational and inspirational readings, some of which were loosely referenced in this memoir.

The Bible
Living Synergistically by Thomas D. Willhite
Loving What Is, Revised Edition: Four Questions That Can Change Your Life by Byron Katie
The Power of Time Perception: Control the Speed of Time to Make Every Second Count
by Jean Paul Zogby
Power Through Constructive Thinking by Emmet Fox
Brief Answers to the Big Questions by Stephen Hawking
The Power of Now: A Guide to Spiritual Enlightenment by Eckhart Tolle
Tertium Organum by P.D. Ouspensky
The Power of Your Subconscious Mind by Joseph Murphy
Realizing Prosperity: Harnessing the Unlimited Power of the Universe to Achieve Your Life's Dreams by Franklin Fillmore Farrington
The Impersonal Life by Joseph Benner
Waking the Tiger: Healing Trauma by Peter A. Levine, Ann Frederick
Reverse the Curse in Your Body and Emotions by Annette Capps
Riches Within Your Reach! by Robert Collier
Healing from Trauma: A Survivor's Guide to Understanding Your Symptoms and Reclaiming Your Life by Jasmin Lee Cori
The Seat of the Soul by Gary Zukav

Mary's Note: When I read any book on the subject of "how to", I listen with my breath. I will know if it was meant for me or not. I'm fond of a proverb that has been attributed to Lao Tzu: *"When the student is ready, a teacher will appear."*